Ron & Jin,

You had earned wonderful talked. This book is about investment success. Readers can learn how to build wealth, and be reminded of deeper truths.

You're wise enough to recognize that material success alone is too small a life goal. Money is a great slave, but a horrid master.

Instead, legacy is a more worthy objective. Legacy is what people think, say, and do because of your influence. Legacy is created by living out your values — by improving others' lives.

These chapters encourage investors to lead lives worth imitating.

May you continue to create and enjoy outrageous success!

APRIL 2023

Praise for

Building Legacy Wealth

"Terry's book is a proven recipe for financial success. We have been friends for 30+ years and I have followed his recipe for acquiring apartment properties and renovating them and have done so with more than 1,000 apartments in San Diego County. And I have passed on his secret sauce to hundreds of my students at UCSD Extension over the years and, they, too, have prospered and benefited from his wisdom."

—Alan Nevin
Author of *The Great Divide*

"Rental housing is a unique business. With a minimal investment you can leverage an asset to archive returns far beyond your outlay. It's also a business that needs to be managed with clear objectives. This book walks all investors from novices through seasoned masters along a path others have successfully traveled. *Building Legacy Wealth*, by Terry Moore, CCIM allows the reader to learn valuable business lessons from others on their road to financial independence."

—Bob Pinnegar
President & CEO of the National Apartment Association

"I have worked with hundreds of commercial real estate brokers, many who are some of the top-performing professionals in the world. Even among them, Terry Moore stands out.

It is obvious that Terry's calling is to help his clients create wealth, through decision-based real estate investments. He challenges himself and his clients to be intentional and to make lifetime choices that will matter when we are all gone.

"Terry will share with you how to make a fortune, but he is more interested in helping you make a long lasting and positive difference. Spend time with the ideas in this book. The people around you will be glad you did."

—Rod Santomassimo, CCIM
Founder and President, Massimo Group, LLC

"You are in for a treat! Terry has distilled the wisdom and the value of multifamily real estate investment to its essence. He presents that concentrated knowledge here in this thoughtful, powerful, and accessible read. For more than a generation our firm has helped Terry, Sandy, and their clients profitably implement the strategies he discusses. Enjoy and prosper!"

—Joe Greenblat, CPM
CEO Sunrise Management, International Past President of the Institute of Property Management (IREM)

"A value-based approach to investing, and a value-based approach to life. The integrated concepts embodied in this book encompass a life well lived through knowledge-based investing and enhancing the quality of lives and community."

—Rick Snyder
President R. A. Snyder Properties
Past President of the California Apartment Association
Past President of the California Association of Realtors™

"Terry expertly describes your life, challenges, lessons, and emotions as a landlord from your first thoughts of investment, through wealth escalation to the passing of your successful financial legacy to your family. And he does it all with heartfelt insights about the people you will interact with along the way."

—Steve Morris
Author of *Leadership Simple* and *Leading People to Lead Themselves*

"Terry Moore is a savant when it comes to investing in apartments, and he has distilled 30 years of knowledge, expertise, and hard work into an easy-to-follow book that will launch the novice or fast-track the more experienced investor. His approach distills advice to make wise investment decisions as well as wise life decisions."

—Jack Crittenden
President & Editor in Chief, *Our City*

"Terry Moore has a wealth of experience that leads to meaningful insights. The industry is fortunate he committed them to paper."

"Real estate brokers who write books are dangerous. Those who know the issues and can clearly express solutions are rare. Terry Moore is one of these."

—Roger J Brown, PhD
Author of *Private Real Estate Investment: Digital Analysis and Decision Making*

"This book is a captivating blend of practical steps to building wealth for generations and solid leadership advice. Terry Moore entertains with his witty phrasing, personal stories, and between-the-eyes challenges to be a better person, smarter investor, and action taker. He sagely shares with us what it takes to build legacy wealth through investing in apartment buildings. His step-by-step approach helps you realize that this truly could be you! You can become a millionaire if you pay attention to this wise advice."

—Mindy Bortness
Owner of Communication Works, a premier coaching venture

"Terry Moore is more than a Realtor, and this book is more than a how to make money in real estate course. Terry's approach to real estate brokerage comes through clearly in the language and tone of the book. In both cases he is aware of the long-term goal, not just racking up a single huge sale and moving on to the next client, rather he builds relationships as he helps his clients build their wealth. Many of his clients continued to come back to him deal after deal, in a business where clients seldom have much loyalty."

—Andy French
Master CREIA Inspector

"This book is like The Millionaire Next Door for the small apartment investor. A must read "

—Pete Smith
Former Principal of Sunrise Management

"I appreciate the relatable story telling that makes Terry's stewardship easy to digest sometimes complicated concepts. I've read my share of books on investing in residential real estate and few make it as understandable as this example. Further, his comments on Legacy Wealth is notable. In my experience, the most successful investors/owners have personal missions that include both financial and personal growth goals and have woven them together."

—Alan Pentico
Executive Director
San Diego County Apartment Association

"Terry is other focused, that is on you and your financial welfare."

—Kent Porter
Author of *Fix Frustrations at Work: Short Stores Empowering You to Make the Difference*

"You have given considerable thought to the subjects at hand. There is a wise and calm tone that is conveyed. Your decency clearly comes across."

—James Graham
Attorney who represents trust attorneys

"A ton of good advice."

—Wally Stevens
  MAI with 40 years' success appraising San Diego apartments

"Great project!"

—Alan Clopine, CPA
  Pure Financial

"I have known and done business with Terry since the mid-1990s, when many of the apartment purchases at that time were REO properties. From a lender's perspective, I appreciate that he always lays out the full scope of the transaction up front—pros and cons. This way all parties know how to approach the deal and structure the financing. He understands lenders' concerns, and will often present a creative approach to putting a transaction together that satisfies the concerns of all parties. I have enjoyed closing many loans with Terry throughout the years.

Terry does his research in understanding the goals of his clients, their investment comfort levels, management experience or inexperience, etc., and finds the appropriate property to match those needs. Terry knows the San Diego neighborhoods and can advise a buyer as to the future planned growth and development of an area they are considering. He will address whether a property needs work and has potential for increased rents, and will advise accordingly. He considers short-term and long-term goals.

Terry is also forthcoming in sharing his experience from being in the business many years. His faith guides his principles. He is a valued and trustworthy resource for both the novice and sophisticated investor."

—Laurie Blake
  Commercial Real Estate Loan Officer
  Mission Federal Credit Union
  CCIM Affiliate Member and Director

Building Legacy Wealth

Building Legacy Wealth

TOP SAN DIEGO APARTMENT BROKER SHOWS
HOW TO BUILD WEALTH
AND LEAD A LIFE WORTH IMITATING

TERRY MOORE, CCIM

Building Legacy Wealth: Building Legacy Wealth: Top San Diego Apartment Broker Shows How to Build Wealth and Lead a Life Worth Imitating

This publication is designed to provide accurate and authoritative information in regard to the subject matter covered and is believed to be correct at the time of writing. The publisher and the author make no representations or warranties with respect to the accuracy or completeness of the contents of this work and specifically disclaim all warranties including without limitation warranties of fitness for a particular purpose. Since every situation is different and laws and regulations vary by jurisdiction and change from time to time, you should seek competent professional counsel before making any decision.

Published by: Legacy Wealth Press
2635 Camino del Rio S. #300
San Diego, CA 92108

ISBNs
Hardcover: 978-1-7321969-0-2
Softcover: 978-1-7321969-1-9
eBook: 978-1-7321969-2-6

Printed in the United States of America

Cover and Interior design: 1106 Design

Contents

Foreword

You are holding an amazing tool designed to ensure your financial well-being, a path for your children, and an opportunity to make a positive impact in our basic need for housing. Congratulations on your time researching a different path to a better future.

Where was this book thirty years ago as I was starting my career in commercial real estate? The knowledge imparted here could have shortened my learning curve considerably.

Terry's advice was pertinent 30 years ago, it's completely relevant today, and I believe it will be for decades to come. You'll see that as he follows a multigeneration family of investors who demonstrate the basic principles of investing and leaving a legacy for others.

Many books are available to tell you the how of investing. The technical skills are not that hard, and so authors abound. It takes an extraordinary individual to frame that knowledge in a bigger picture that will positively impact your life and the lives of those you touch. Terry Moore is uniquely qualified as that rare individual.

Terry "walks the talk." He knows his stuff and practices it daily. But where he differentiates himself is in the generous sharing of his expertise.

Terry counsels clients, sells real estate, owns and manages income property, and helps other do it. His moral compass is unerring: His client's needs *always* come first.

Terry makes a positive difference in the community. Not only has he attained the CCIM (Certified Commercial Investment Member) designation, he served on the national CCIM faculty, an even rarer distinction. He has also taught for the California Association of Realtors, National University's Real Estate MBA program, and UCSD's Extension Program. When he represents a client, the offers he writes go to the top of the stack due to his credibility with the brokerage community and lenders. That credibility comes from decades of closing transactions in a calm, business-like manner, encyclopedic knowledge of the market, and terrific problem solving. He has the full backing, support, and wise advice of his wife, Sandy, and he has assembled a team dedicated to his clients' success.

My only regret in this business is the buildings I should have purchased. Terry's wise counsel will help you avoid that regret. My life and career are better for having Terry and Sandy in it. Yours can be, too, with the sage recommendations contained within these pages.

—Ann Block, CCIM
Closed more than $4 billion of income property sales and loans. Lifetime Achievement Award by San Diego County Apartment Association, Woman of Influence *Real Estate Forum* magazine
17-time national award winner for Chase and Washington Mutual apartment loan production.
Only Loan Advisor to train and promote more than four other people who also became national award-winning producers.
Past President of San Diego County Apartment Association
Past President of San Diego CCIM Certified Commercial Investment Member chapter
CCIM Designee of Year, San Diego County CCIM chapter

Preface to the Revised Edition

WELCOME TO THE SILVER AGE of California apartment investing!

California's economic environment is superior to about 40 other states. California and most of its major cities have grown faster than the rest of the nation and most other states for two generations. State housing and tax policies created a huge, pent-up demand for rental housing. It may take a decade or more for the construction industry to build enough to bring markets back into balance. From about 1980 till about 2020 the state may not have built even half as many apartments as the population needed. That supply-and-demand imbalance boosted values and made millions of California investors millionaires.

Silver age . . . what happened to the golden age?

You just missed it. Since I wrote this book in 2018, there have been three significant changes that affect apartment investing.

First, California imposed rent control even though voters rejected the idea 3 to 2. Nationally one-third of renters live in rent control housing. Rent control does not create additional housing. Also, rent control also doesn't eliminate profit, cash flow, or wealth building.

California's rent control law restricts most rental increases to 5% plus the local cost of living. For owners of San Diego rentals in 2020 that's effectively about a 7% increase. The maximum increase is 10% annually, regardless of the annual cost of living. The law makes an exception when the owner makes substantial improvements, which the law indicates include:

- Intent to obtain building permits,
- expectation that the work will take more than 30 days,
- cannot be performed with the tenant in place, and
- will involve major work to the plumbing and or electrical system

Second, the state government changed law to create more rental housing, taking the power of "No" away from local jurisdictions. The laws promote more density, including construction of additional dwelling units (ADUs), previously called "granny flats." For a generation, the state told local jurisdictions to allow more housing, particularly rental housing. Local jurisdictions ignored the state. The state now forces local jurisdictions to allow ADUs.

The density bonus laws represent a five-year opportunity for rental owners and entrepreneurs. The law, which was passed in October 2019, gives homeowners and rental owners the right, by law, to add more units. The local jurisdiction has 60 days to approve the application for those units. A cottage industry has sprung up to advise owners and developers on the implications of that law. Hundreds of brokers are scrambling to maximize our clients' benefits. Like it or not, the density bonus law won't sunset until the end of 2025.

Third, during the COVID-19 pandemic, California, in effect, made rental owners "the lender of first resort" for renters. The state effectively barred evictions for nonpayment for several months and the implications may last for a year. Rental owners are aware that convenience store owners and gas station operators were not compelled to make interest-free loans to customers. Tenants who pay no rent from September 1, 2010 till January

30, 2021, but who pay 25% of what they owe on January 31, 2021, cannot be evicted for being late.

The California Supreme Court or federal court may rule on the interpretation and implementation of these laws. Until then a fabulous investment broker may provide guidance beyond what's obvious as of the date this edition goes to press.

You and I can't change the trends or predict with certainty what the governor, legislature, and/or the courts will do. We decide whether we'll invest in our areas code or move our funds to another metro or maybe another time zone. Thousands of California investors are selling their rental properties and moving the equity to other places where the politics match their worldview more closely. Expect that trend to continue through most of the 2020s. That will create a moderately higher property turnover. By 2030 most investors who don't like progressive politics will have moved most of their equity to other places.

—TERRY MOORE, CCIM
    San Diego, California
    December 2020

Preface

SEVERAL YEARS AGO, I DECIDED NOT TO WRITE A BOOK. My best male friend suggested we write a book together, but we had two problems. We shared many interests, but we didn't share much expertise and we couldn't clearly identify the potential readers. We shelved that idea and moved on to other adventures, but the book writing seed had been planted in my mind.

The book writing seed was there as I read hundreds of books about how to set and achieve worthwhile goals, create wealth, minimize risk, think and act with emotional intelligence, develop and use leverage and intelligence wisely, and positively impact others. Many books were insightful, but some made better doorstops than guides to wise decision making.

The seed began to germinate as I served my clients and advised other wealthy investors. Over the last generation I have answered investment real estate questions, explained realities, and presented insights hundreds of times. Most potential investors have some interesting fantasies unsupported by reality. Part of my job as a broker is to help people understand market reality and what their options are.

Since I want my clients to become wise investors, I've developed what are now proven and repeatable processes to build wealth and live lives worth imitating. Clients have benefited from clarifying their values and goals, assessing opportunities, and making wise buying, operating, and selling decisions. Hundreds of clients have become millionaires, and scores have become multimillionaires using those processes.

Many wise investors choose apartment investing because it can be a low-risk escalator to wealth. The math is steady and powerful. However, there is more than math involved. Landlording is face-to-face capitalism. It offers you the opportunity to make a difference in the lives of others as you build your wealth. Those thoughts incubated as I worked to help my clients.

Two years ago, after several radio interviews and industry speeches, I mentioned to my wife, Sandy, that I was inclined to write a book. Sandy's profound question was "What will you say that is different from other get-rich-in-real-estate books?" We realized that writing about how to get rich was too small a goal and that a worthier objective was to help readers achieve wealth and significance. Most people eventually realize that relationships and impact on others are more important accomplishments than building wealth alone.

The book had to be easy to understand and provide practical steps that would enable investors to progress toward their worthy goals. Here are some important things I hope to articulate:

- Why some people who aspire to wealth should never be rental owners and why others, with less income or education or capital, thrive as landlords.

- The difference between the minority of novice investors who actually buy investment property and the majority of equally financially capable people who never close escrow.

- How to identify your best financial and life goals.

- How to build a great team to accomplish your financial goals.

- How to identify and capture the best available options.

- How to maximize wealth once you're a property owner.

- An instant wealth building tool that amplifies profits in San Diego and other supply constrained markets.

- How to balance the goals of maximizing your wealth while minimizing your risk.

- How to know when to reinvest and how to wisely repeat your superior success.

- How to avoid investment mistakes that smart people make.

- How to improve the value of the housing stock, which benefits the residents and also builds wealth in a low-risk way.

- The difference between legacy and inheritance.

- The many ways you can do good while doing well.

- How to increase the chance of your family's adopting your values and not merely inheriting your estate.

- How to increase your chance of significance as you become more successful.

Sandy affirmed that the topics were worth knowing, that I had a superior track record of conveying those issues, and that a well-written book would be worthwhile. Then we talked about who I wanted to read the book.

Over the years, people in various stages of financial maturity had thanked me for helping them make wise choices. If what follows describes you, then I wrote this book for you.

I wrote the book for you if you're a hardworking person or couple with $200K in investable assets, along with the desire to become a millionaire. This book can help you investigate the potential and trade-offs of apartment investing so you can make a wise decision about whether it will be the way you choose to build legacy wealth.

I wrote this book for you if you already own some rentals, perhaps two to five homes or condos . . . or maybe you're on your second building above five units. You have deposited rent checks and have benefited from inflation. You have some experience, and you recognize that others have greater expertise in important areas. You're ready to learn more. Many of my clients started where you are. I wrote this book for you, too.

If you're already a millionaire landlord, you have different challenges. Maybe, like many of my clients, you have more wealth than your family needs for the next fifty years. As a market-proven master, you want to imprint following generations with values that will be as important as, or maybe more important than, the wealth. I wrote this book for you.

I also wrote the book for me—forty years ago. I wish these lessons had come sooner and cheaper. I've learned a lot the hard way. I've tried to select and clearly present the concepts that are most likely to help you. In money matters, prudent risk taking is vital. This volume guides you toward taking *only* prudent risks.

This book is not about how to get rich quick, and it's not just about building wealth steadily. It's also about what writer David Brooks termed "the eulogy virtues," the things others will talk about at your memorial service, what people will do and be able to do because you were here.

Your legacy, the imprint you leave on the world, is worth your attention. The book is seasoned with paragraphs about topics more important than simply making your money multiply.

With silver hair, too many mistakes, and a generation of striving to help winners achieve more, my perspective has changed. I don't have it all together, but I may be able to guide you toward effective ways to live out your life purpose.

By aspiring to wealth, you are also aspiring to be a person of impact, to have influence, to be a leader. Maybe you've been a leader since childhood, or maybe you've never thought of yourself as a leader. Rental owners are leaders, whether they recognize it or not.

Rental owners impact others' lives in profound ways. Some people might choose you as a role model. Since you're going to be a leader, do it with excellence and on purpose. Martin Luther King Jr. challenged people, if you're going to be street sweeper, be the best street sweeper you can. These pages will invite and challenge you to become the person you were created to be . . . someone more impactful and more successful than you are now.

My friend Ian started out as a protégé more than a decade ago. He reminded me a lot of how I was at the same age. He's become very successful in real estate investment, and our original relationship has grown into a deep and trusting friendship between men who seek excellence in our craft. Monthly we have breakfast to sharpen and bless each other.

At one of our breakfasts, I was describing this project when he looked at me across the table and asked, "To what end?"

My friend was asking a heart question; he wanted to know, and he wanted me to think about my motivation. Years ago, one of the nicest things my loving wife ever said was "You have nothing left to prove."

So why did it seem as if I was trying to prove more things? Part of my reason is rooted in my faith. My understanding of the Abrahamic covenant is that my gifts are only important to the extent that they help other people. I pondered that and several other things.

There was close to a minute of silence. Do you have any idea how long a minute of silence is?

"To what end?" my buddy asked again.

I told him that my heart wanted to invite other successful investors to make a positive, long-lasting impact. My calling includes helping successful people accomplish what they might not do without me. That's also the deep reason that I wrote this book. May this book enable you to more effectively build your wealth and legacy. The objective is not merely to make you wealthier but, more importantly, to increase the likelihood that you'll lead a life worth imitating.

—TERRY MOORE, CCIM
San Diego, California
February 2018

Introduction

> "Virtue does not come from wealth, but . . . wealth, and every
> other good thing which men have . . . comes from virtue."
> —Socrates

BETTY AND PAUL MARRIED IN 1940. They worked hard and started a family. Early on they acquired some rental property. They lived frugally, managed their properties sensibly, and added more. When they died, they were multimillionaires. Their offspring are respectable, responsible, and financially independent rental owners. This book is about how you can do what they did.

Like Paul and Betty, most of us don't begin life as rich people. Instead, we acquire our wealth over time with hard work, good habits, and maybe some insight and luck. Hundreds of our clients were the first millionaires in their family. Many of their kids may became decamillionaires. Two of my clients are billionaires; billionaires are rare. More than 90% of my clients who became millionaires invested in apartments.

Why So Many Real Estate Millionaires Do It with Apartments

Author and speaker Jack Canfield likes to say that "success leaves clues." Most real estate investors start out by owning rental condos or rental houses. Many folks "graduate to apartments" because apartment investing has an incredible upside.

Seven Reasons Why Investing in Apartments Can Make You a Millionaire

Seven truths that favor rental owners can help you become a millionaire and build your legacy. The seventh truth is most powerful and especially applicable in supply-constrained markets such as San Diego, California.

1. **Leverage**

   Almost everyone who buys real estate uses leverage. It is rare that people save all the money for their home before they buy. Instead, most households save enough for a down payment, buy, and then a generation later pay it off. The home almost always increases in value between the purchase date and the date the loan is paid off. The homeowner benefits from the appreciation that accrued from the date of purchase to the date that the home is sold or the loan is paid off.

   Similarly, most investors obtain a prudent loan. Almost none pay all cash. Look at the math. Suppose you have $300K for investment and were deciding between buying a rental house or some apartments. Also suppose that values increase 10% over time. The $300K house could be worth $330K. The $1 million apartment could be worth $1.1 million. After paying off the $700K loan, the leveraged equity would have grown to $400K for the apartment. Clearly, $400K equity is better than $330K.

2. **Cash flow**

   Many people focus on this measurement: "How much cash do I receive after all expenses and paying the mortgage?" It is simple to calculate but far less important than growth of capital. Most investors don't consider the tax refunds that usually come from owning rental property.

Over the past 25 years, initial cash return on the invested capital (often called the *cash-on-cash return*) has varied from 2% since 2017 up to a peak of 10% during San Diego's most severe recession. Generally, cash flow increases over the years. Rent increases while the mortgage remains the same.

Initially the investment's cash flow is weak and uneven. With passing years, the rents increase. Suppose gross income increased 10% from $100K to $110K. The mortgage payment is fixed, and increases in other costs are relatively small. The owners' cash flow might increase $7.5K. Many rental owners find that their property generates more cash flow than all their other retirement and social security combined.

3. **Tax shelter**

Apartment investors pay lower income taxes because a tax fiction called *depreciation* implies that residential buildings become valueless in 30 years in the 2017 tax law. If you don't own income property, you may not know that the government subsidizes landlords by giving extra tax deductions, which, in effect, means extra refunds.

A rough example is that if a $1 million building only breaks even in terms of income and expense, the owner can claim a taxable loss of $25K. That means the owner can offset, or shelter, $25K of ordinary income. Depending on your tax bracket and state, it might mean $5K to $10K in tax refunds for owning rentals.

4. **Inflation protection through appreciation**

Democracies vote benefits to more and more people. Currency is printed and inflation happens. In the last hundred years, U.S. inflation has averaged 3% per year. So last decade's $1 million building can be worth $1.3 million or more now.

5. **Mortgage pay-down**

   Each mortgage payment has interest and principal reduction. After a decade, the loan may be 20% paid, yet after two decades it may be half paid. In 30 years the loan is gone. In other words, the tenants make your mortgage payments. Once the loan is paid off, then you keep all the cash flow.

6. **Tax-deferred exchange**

   In effect, a savvy investor can trade up and receive an interest-free loan from the government and have the equity compound for decades; the family may never have to pay that tax liability.

   With income property, you can sell an asset, buy or "exchange into" another one, but not have to pay the taxes on the appreciation at time of sale. Instead, the tax is deferred to the time when you sell the last property you "exchanged into." This is not true for stocks or bonds. When you die, your heirs receive the property based on its value at date of death. In effect, tax-deferred exchange may allow you to disinherit the tax authority and eliminate the tax liability on the accumulated profit.

7. **Monetize your cash flow**

   You may have heard about initial public offerings, IPOs. Tech geeks bring the company to the stock exchange, and they sell it for 10, 20, or maybe 100 times earnings. In effect, they are selling an income stream. The market values apartments at a multiple of rents: 5, 10, or 20 times the annual rental income. So, $1K of additional rental income increases the value of the property by many times.

   Improving a property increases its value. In most counties, putting $10K of improvement adds $5K of value. Relatively few people seek out markets with low returns. Generally, metropolitan areas not growing as fast as the national average have higher risk but no chance of superior upside. Piddling demand and ample supply means higher vacancy rates, limited growth in rents, and restricted appreciation potential. Places with stable or decreasing population are unacceptable risks for almost all investors. Values will shrink; the questions are merely when and by how much.

By contrast, in places such as San Diego, ordinary investors may be able to make $15,000 of improvement and raise the rents 15% and create $20K–$25K of extra value. All investors would prefer to have $15K return rather than $5K. Supply-constrained markets offer a power tool, a force multiplier, which makes apartment investing especially appealing. This tool is especially powerful in markets with immense demand and limits to new construction.

Those seven powerful incentives help real estate investors. Other factors make apartment investing an especially attractive way to build wealth.

The market for apartment investments offers many opportunities for you to build wealth. This volume aims to serve investors in many markets. Many of the examples will draw on San Diego reality, but you will find value in the book, even though your county differs from San Diego.

Residential income property has less risk than commercial building. Not every person needs a commercial space. Commercial space is far more expensive to customize for each business tenant; many jurisdictions require building permits to make tenant improvements for commercial space. In contrast, few governments demand permits to rerent apartment units. Commercial space takes longer to lease vacancy and has higher risk during tough times. In recessions, many businesses downsize or die. In contrast, families don't die, but they may tighten their belts.

Recessions aren't the only extra risk to commercial property. Changing technology disrupts society. Existing buildings, like shopping malls, warehouses, and office buildings, are vulnerable because of the technological disruptions, such as how the growth of Internet commerce changes the economics of retail and warehouse space and telecommuting reduces demand for office space.

An investor with $50K can buy a rental house, but not a shopping mall. That rental house can start the investor on the road to legacy wealth. Perhaps a third of our clients began with a rental house or condo and then graduated to apartments.

Market forces make apartment investing attractive, but government policies also favor apartment owners.

Savvy apartment investors know that the government favors apartment investing over other forms of investing in several ways. Current tax law favors residential real estate with faster depreciation, 30 years, compared to commercial's 39.5 years. Banking regulations treat residential lending as half the risk of industrial, office, or retail. Because of the regulations, lenders make more and cheaper loans for residential than for commercial properties.

Real estate experts consider apartment markets balanced when the vacancy rate is near 5%. San Diego's apartment vacancy rate has averaged between 3–4% for more than a decade. When demand exceeds supply, prices increase, and San Diego rents have outpaced inflation the last generation. Investing in apartments, especially in a supply-constrained market like San Diego, is a proven way to build wealth, but this book is about more than that. You can learn more about supply-constrained markets in Appendix A, Supply and Demand.

Legacy Wealth

This book is about building legacy wealth. Legacy wealth is more important than merely getting rich. Legacy is what people do, say, and think because of your influence. Your legacy is already occurring. Legacy starts before you die. Betty and Paul's legacy starts with their children.

Betty and Paul taught their children the landlording trade. Their children became good and successful landlords and astute investors.

The parents also modeled balanced lives. Paul made time for a couple of buddies, and Betty stayed close to her friends. They also showed how to deal with emotional, irrational, and drunken tenants. The kids saw how to make peace with neighbors who have different expectations. They also listened and learned that most people keep the promises they make. But they also learned that some people made promises that were quickly forgotten, and they saw how their parents responded.

All the children learned life lessons about attending to actions, discounting words; planning and following through; exercising patience, prudence, and tact; and so much more. Those kids, who are now grandparents, have emotional intelligence, and they value people. They are wise, frugal, and generous.

Paul and Betty prepared their children to be prudent investors and stellar human beings. But their legacy doesn't stop there. Their legacy extends to all the people who rent from the family or who work for them to maintain their quality rentals. That must be at least a thousand people.

I'm among the many people who have been blessed by Betty and Paul's legacy. They and their children have taught me important lessons. Building legacy wealth can enrich your life. There's no magic; it does require a lot of hard work and discipline.

Betty and Paul weren't exceptionally smart or educated. They began with a good work ethic and common sense. They acquired their first property and built from there. They worked hard and learned as they went along. They also left a potent legacy. There are several ways you can leave a legacy, and Paul and Betty demonstrated all of them.

Your legacy involves more than the inheritance you leave. Paul and Betty's inheritance gave their children choices they wouldn't have had otherwise. Other clients I serve will leave some of their wealth to their church, synagogue, alma mater, or causes they supported in life.

Your legacy is the example you set. Paul and Betty worked hard and lived frugally. They modeled how to deal with people, even difficult people.

Your legacy includes the lessons you teach. Paul and Betty set examples of good behavior, but they also taught some lessons explicitly. Their daughter, Jeanie, remembers one:

> We were taught that we were never better than anyone else, regardless of race, creed, religion, gender, anything. My mom told us over and over that we should never criticize another person until we had "walked a mile in his moccasins."

Your legacy will be how you lived and how the choices you made affected the lives of others. Paul and Betty were landlords who improved their properties, giving their tenants a better quality of life and improving the neighborhoods where they invested. Their children learned and applied those lessons. They have chosen to build their legacy wealth by owning rental property.

Should You Be a Rental Owner?

Rental ownership is face-to-face capitalism. If you are a landlord, you or your property management team will deal with tenants. Most of those dealings will be pleasant. Some will not.

Someday a tenant will need to be evicted because they're not a good neighbor. Someone, maybe you, will have to talk with them and say "You can't throw your cigarette butts over the balcony any longer. You can't play loud music at 3:00 AM any longer. If you're going to live here, that is not a permissible activity."

Landlords and property managers may have conversations about home, family, culture, neighborliness, and appropriate adult behavior in a community. Most people will never need to talk with another adult outside their family about moving the headboard an inch away from the wall, to prevent it from disturbing the people in the next apartment. Yet there may be times when someone needs to explain what consideration means and how to ensure a neighbor's quiet enjoyment.

You'll discover that most problems with tenant behavior aren't self-healing, and the longer you put off a difficult conversation the harder it will be. Many of those conversations deal with people in crisis, and that gives you an opportunity to build your legacy. Here's how one of Paul and Betty's adult children describes a common situation:

> One of our tenants had a family emergency. Her parent died, and she needed to go to Texas by bus. And I worked out a thing where she paid part of her rent and then she'd pay me $100 extra a month until it was resolved. Some people make good on that. Some people don't. But I choose to give people a little bit of the benefit of the doubt, especially people who've had a lot of disadvantages in their life.

Rental ownership offers you opportunities to build your legacy while you build your wealth. This book will give you the tools you need, but only you can decide if apartment investing is right for you. If it is, here's how this book will help you.

What's in This Book

The meat of the book is in four sections: Increase the Odds of Your Success, Prepare to Invest Profitably in Apartments, The Wealth Escalator, and Your Investment Life Trajectory. The seasoning of this book is legacy. Your legacy, goals, and values differ from those of the next reader and from mine. Great: You were created for some unique purpose. If you're going to be a rental owner, then let's help you move closer to the best version of that future you, the most inspiring, the most worthy of imitation.

When I work with clients, I tell them it's up to them to decide where they want to go and how fast they want to get there. My job is to be their guide and navigator.

Think about your legacy in whatever way you find comfortable. Some people use the language of science or business. Other people use faith words. Tune in to the voice that speaks to you.

Increase the Odds of Your Success

This section sets the stage before specific investment strategies are discussed. The chapters on wealthy thinking and emotional intelligence are worth skimming for all readers. Some of us have not yet mastered all these powerful concepts. There is a chapter on understanding what's important to you. Doing the work to clarify your priorities will help you make wise investment decisions quickly enough to capture fleeting opportunities.

Prepare to Invest Profitably in Apartments

This section will help you become a successful apartment investor. Some investors might be tempted to skip this section because they don't understand its importance. That would be a mistake.

Find a broker who will make a great partner. That is a key to achieving the most through your apartment investing. Then, you and your broker must either select or develop a system that works for you every time you invest. Wise investors build legacy wealth by stringing together a series of successful investments; and powerful, repeatable processes help you do that.

You'll also learn how to develop your own understanding of the market and various submarkets. Your broker should be an expert advisor, but you need a sense of what a good investment looks like. You'll discover some realities of apartment investing that give many investors trouble.

The Wealth Escalator

These chapters describe a proven system for successfully assessing opportunities and then successfully buying, operating, and selling investment property. Another chapter highlights a section of the IRS code designed to promote economic growth, allowing investors to build legacy wealth more rapidly by legally paying less income tax.

Your Investment Life Trajectory

This section begins with a chapter titled Prolonging Your Capital's Growth Spurt, where you'll learn how to adjust your strategy to changing life circumstances and goals. The chapter titled Moving On describes four common options if your transition moves on from apartment investing.

The final chapter is Transferring Your Legacy Wealth. Many people have built fortunes, only to have them disappear within a generation or two. You'll learn why it happens and how you can be the exception. You'll discover how Paul and Betty's example can be a template for applying proven wealth-transfer strategies.

For decades I've been studying and serving wealthy people of character who live lives worth imitating. Since before I earned my MBA, I've helped adults make smart choices about money and about topics more important that wealth. These pages are my best gleanings so far.

Just one more thing before you turn the page: What you're about to learn is not any kind of "secret." It isn't magic. And it isn't the only way to become wealthy. But it *is* proven. Over the last generation, I've helped hundreds of families become millionaires with this approach. They are heroes to their family and friends.

Read what's here, and then do one thing more: Apply what you learn. You can be a hero, too.

The next chapter will help you begin your own hero's journey, depending on your starting point.

How to Get the Most from This Book

"We only truly know a thing when we can apply
it to get results."
—MICHAEL POLANYI

"It's not the will to win that matters.
It's the will to prepare to win that matters."
—BEAR BRYANT

"Learn every day, but especially from the experiences
of others. It's cheaper!"
—JOHN BOGLE

MY APARTMENT INVESTING JOURNEY BEGAN about 40 years ago. It wasn't very auspicious. I went to a seminar put on by a real estate broker who urged people to buy small apartment buildings. I scoffed at what he had to say. I was arrogant and believed that I knew better. Shortly after that, Sandy and I moved out of state to buy a business. We decided to rent out the house we had been living in. That was my first landlording experience, and I wasn't very good at it.

Six years later, we moved back to San Diego, and I had a rude shock. I discovered that the people who'd heeded that broker's advice to invest in apartments had tripled their equity in the time that I was gone.

That got my attention, and I remembered an insight I'd had earlier. I was working for the world's largest bank as a commercial loan officer and serving millionaires. I noticed that the people who were in the service business and were good and lucky became wealthy. The people who were in retailing who were smart, good, and lucky became wealthy. It was the same for people who did manufacturing. My only clients who were dumb and unlucky, and still wealthy, were the real estate junkies.

After working as a partner in a real estate development firm for a year, I began the serious part of my apartment investing journey in 1996. Sandy and I bought a seven-unit foreclosure with $60K down. We didn't do it alone; we partnered with people who knew and trusted us, and a client. They and the experience taught me a lot.

At that point in my life, I knew two things. I'd seen the potential of apartment investing as a low-risk escalator to wealth. I'd also learned how much I didn't know and how much I needed to learn if I wanted to achieve my goals. More than 30 years later, I'm writing this book as a way to help you achieve your goals through low-risk apartment investing.

This book can be your roadmap to legacy wealth. The journey you take will be unique. That's because you are unique and your situation is unique. But, you'll be taking roads many other people have taken before you. The exact route you take depends on your starting point.

This chapter describes four positions or roles on the legacy-wealth journey. From each position, the "reading road map" will help you get the most out of this book and help you progress. I've used the names originated by the medieval craft guilds to represent levels of competence: novice, apprentice, journeyman, and master. Thanks to Ken Blanchard for teaching me this learning model.

These are not discrete categories. They blend into each other. And, there's no right answer about where to start. Pick the starting point that seems most like your situation, and then use the reading roadmap I provide to help you get the most from this book. At each role or position, your goal is to move to the next stage.

Novice

If you've never cashed a rent check, you're a novice. That's how we all start. I was a novice for a long time until I decided that rental ownership was the right choice for me, and I've helped clients who were novices become successful apartment investors.

When I met siblings Maria, Juan, and Jose they were novices. They each owned their own homes, but not one of them had $50K of liquid assets. They each refinanced their homes and came up with a total of about $250K, which they used to buy a fourplex. If you're a novice, you need to do two things.

First, decide if apartment investing is a good choice for you. If it is, then you must assess how ready you are to start investing. Here's your reading roadmap.

- Read the Introduction (if you haven't already).
- Skim the The Wealth Escalator and Your Investment Life Trajectory sections.
- If real estate investing seems like a good choice for you, read the section titled Increase the Odds of Your Success. One key thing you will need to do is assess your readiness to invest. For that, flip to Appendix B, Are You Ready to Invest?

Siblings Maria, Juan, and Jose decided they wanted to progress along the apartment wealth-building route. They closed on their first property and cashed their first rent check. They were on their way to being apprentices.

Apprentice

Apprentices have started on the road to building legacy wealth through low-risk apartment investing. Maybe they bought a bigger home and their earlier home became "the rent house." Many apprentices are accidental landlords. Maybe they've inherited a building and realize that they must learn how to manage it well and turn it into more money. Being an accidental landlord or closing on your first property doesn't make you an apprentice until you've tried to do something with it.

You're an apprentice if you've bought and sold more than one investment property and if you've upgraded more than one. You may have already learned the important lesson that the money you spend on upgrades is almost wasted unless either the rents go up or the costs go down. That's the only way that value can increase.

You're an apprentice if you have some experience as an apartment investor and landlord but don't have a clear strategy for riding the escalator to wealth that apartment investing can be. I'll give you the tools to develop a strategy. Here's your reading roadmap:

- Read the Introduction (if you haven't already).
- Skim The Wealth Escalator and the Your Investment Life Trajectory sections.
- Read the section titled Increase the Odds of Your Success.
- Check out Appendix B, Are You Ready to Invest?
- When you're ready, team up with a great broker.
- Use this book as a handbook.

When I first began working with Mark and Sharon, they were apprentices. They owned two rentals. Since then, we've developed a clear strategy and they've moved up. Today, they own more than 100 units. They've become journeymen.

Journeyman

Journeymen have bought and sold many times. If you're a journeyman, you've probably learned about the power of a 1031 exchange. You've used a broker and maybe even found a great one. I hope you've developed a repeatable system for your investing. You want to master good ways to prioritize opportunities, negotiate successfully to close, operate profitably, upgrade properties, and sell when the time is right.

If you're a journeyman, your challenge is to master the craft. Here's my suggestion for your reading roadmap to help do that:

- Read the Introduction (if you haven't already).

- Skim the section titled Increase the Odds of Your Success.

- Skim The Wealth Escalator and the Your Investment Life Trajectory sections.

- Assess your current brokerage relationship. Make changes if you are not receiving excellent service from a broker who has your best interest at heart.

- Use this book as a handbook.

Master

If you're a master, you are already a successful investor and you probably have an impressive net worth. You're looking for techniques that will make your investing even more effective. Maybe you want your success to turn into significance. You want to keep your growth spurt going, but you're also concerned with your legacy and transferring your wealth and the lessons you can teach the next generation. Here's your reading road map:

- Read the Introduction (if you haven't already).

- Skim the section titled Increase the Odds of Your Success.

🌿 Skim The Wealth Escalator and the Your Investment Life Trajectory sections.

🌿 Read the chapter titled Team Up with a Great Broker, assess your current brokerage relationship, and make changes, if necessary.

🌿 Use this book as a handbook.

If you're a Master, you probably know many things that are here. Feel free to skip those parts.

Here's a chart that summarizes the four positions:

	NOVICE	APPRENTICE	JOURNEYMAN	MASTER
STATUS	Curious	Committed	Competent	Master
PROPERTY TO START	None	Limited	Apartment buildings	Multiple projects
GOALS	Answer the questions "Is this for me?" and "Am I ready?"	Develop an effective property investment strategy	Master the craft of apartment investing	Advance from success to significance

Squeeze the Most Value from Your Reading

Science philosopher Michael Polanyi has said, "We only truly know a thing when we can use it to get a result."

Reading books is great; it's enjoyable and you learn a lot. But I didn't write this book for you to enjoy it or simply learn a lot. I wrote it so you could use it to follow the well-trodden path to legacy wealth. With that in mind, here are some suggestions about how to get the most from this or any book.

I've suggested some reading roadmaps for you, but don't be bound by that or by the Table of Contents at the beginning of the book. Read things in whatever order makes sense to you.

Mark up the book. Highlight important pages. Make notes in the margins.

You'll get many ideas when you're reading. Capture them. If you don't, they will fly away. Keep a notebook, index cards, or a voice recorder handy to capture your ideas.

Take notes or write summaries of chapters. Writing things out in your own way helps you both learn and understand how to apply what you've learned.

Create action lists. Write things down that you can do right away. You won't learn about successful investing from books. You'll only learn by doing—practice, reflect, and repeat.

Make reading a habit. One thing most successful people have in common is that they are voracious and intentional readers. Make that a habit. To help you get started, mine the section, A Brief Annotated Reading List, near the back of the book.

That's it for how to get the most from this book. Get started right away on using your reading road map.

Increase the Odds of Your Success

The three chapters in this section will help you increase the odds of your success in real estate investing and many other areas of your life.

The **Wealthy Thinking** chapter demonstrates how to live like the millionaire next door. You'll learn about living a disciplined and frugal life and about steady, disciplined investing.

The **Emotional Intelligence** chapter can help you succeed in spite of aggravating people and complex situations.

This section's final chapter, **Understand Your Values and Priorities**, enables you to clarify and prioritize what's important to you. That simplifies your decision making and increases your odds of obtaining your most important results.

Wealthy Thinking

"Success is never final; failure is never fatal.
It's the courage to continue that counts."
~ WINSTON CHURCHILL

"A prudent person profits from personal experience,
a wise one from the experience of others."
~ JOSEPH COLLINS

"Chance favors only the prepared mind."
~ LOUIS PASTEUR

I STARTED COMPETING IN TRIATHLONS after I was 60. When some people hear that I participate in triathlons, they think it's really something and that I'm a super-fit competitive athlete. Maybe they're imagining the Iron Man Triathlon that's on TV, where competitors swim a couple of miles, bike 100 miles, and end by running a marathon. I don't do anything close to that. Those are world-class athletes. I do triathlons to stay fit.

A few years ago, I saw something about triathlons and thought, "That looks hard. Could I do that?" I thought, "I can jog. I rarely fall off the bike. And I haven't drowned in the pool yet. Since I can do each piece, then I can probably do them together. It seems like a great way to stay fit so I can live a longer, healthier life. I'll try it."

Winning a triathlon is not my goal. That would be a delight, but I'm realistic about my fitness and my commitment, and I'm pleased to be the best triathlete in my age group in my census tract. My wife, Sandy, is the only other triathlete in our census tract. I'm ahead of millions of others who are SOC, "still on the couch." And when I'm tired and when I'm hurt, and when I'm embarrassed, I cross the finish line, maybe last in my age group, but I last until the finish and end ahead of all those people who are SOC.

My triathlon objective is long-term health, not standing on the medals podium. Once I was the only one in the Methuselah age group and I collected first place because there was no competition. In the next event I was fifth of nine. Likewise, this book is about helping you obtain a better financial result, not about making you the richest person in your state.

This chapter is about wealthy thinking. That's thinking like the millionaire next door, the one who mows his own lawn. You won't become rich like super investors such as Warren Buffet, just as I'm not going to compete against Iron Man triathletes. For you and for me, the objective is to improve to develop our gifts and capital.

Few of us inherited wealth; we built it. If you want to build more wealth safely and steadily, you're more likely to succeed if you think like people who become wealthy.

In this chapter, you'll learn about the kind of trade-offs that will increase your chances of building wealth. You'll discover a principle from a Weight Watchers talk that turns out to be powerful in many areas of life, and you'll learn about the incredible importance of self-discipline. I'll tell you how people who become wealthy think and behave differently from those who don't. You'll learn some ways to increase your own self-discipline and about the role of luck in increasing your odds of financial success. It may not be what you think.

Pick Your Hard

The Weight Watchers program works on two basic truths. One is biological. If you consume more calories than you burn, you will gain weight. If you burn more than you take in, you will lose weight. The other principle is psychological. Success is more likely if you have a simple system to follow, a way to measure how you're doing, and social support. Weight Watchers provides social support through weekly meetings, which include a weigh-in and a motivational talk. One memorable talk was titled, "Pick your hard." Here it is, in a nutshell:

> "Losing weight is hard. Keeping it off is hard. Being obese is hard. Pick your hard!"

Becoming financially independent is hard. Living only on Social Security is hard. Feeble old age is hard. So is staying fit by running triathlons. Doing the things necessary to get rich is hard, but so is not having resources at the end of life. This book is about decisions, big and small. They're mostly financial decisions, but some are character and legacy choices. *Trade-offs* is another way of saying *decisions*. Here's an example.

A friend decided that she wanted to lose another three pounds in the few weeks before Thanksgiving. Having a goal is important, but so is realizing when achieving it won't be easy. This friend had to pay close attention to what she ate and increased her exercise a bit. Her choices weren't fun in the short term, but she achieved her goal.

My friend and her mate often go to a play and normally enjoy a fine restaurant beforehand. That's part of their date-night tradition. That year they skipped the luxury cuisine and chose a lighter, healthier option instead. My friend returned to her goal weight before Thanksgiving. She picked her hard. It's an exercise in self-discipline. At Thanksgiving, this lady celebrated with some of her favorite foods, and the family recognized that she was still the slimmest of the ladies within 30 years of her.

Self-Discipline is the Key to Picking the Right Hard

Wealthy thinking is having the discipline to do things that aren't easy or fun, for long-term gain. That's hard. Most of the time people know what to do. Most of the people who smoke or who are obese know it's not good for them. They probably also know what they should do to quit smoking or lose weight. They're still on the couch, smoking. Their choice costs them vigor now and may reduce their life span by a decade or more.

The science that proves the importance of self-discipline was started in the 1960s with the research of Walter Mischel. Here's the experiment. A kid of four or so was brought into a room where there were yummy treats on a table, usually marshmallows or Oreo cookies. The child could eat one treat now, or whenever he or she wanted. But if the child could hold off eating the treat until the experimenter returned, he or she would be rewarded with three treats. It was hard for the kids.

Only about a third could control their urges. They could hold out longer if the treats were out of sight or if they thought of something "fun." That's interesting, but not nearly as interesting as what Mischel found with a follow-up experiment.

About ten years after the original experiment, Mischel thought it might be interesting to see what happened to the participants in his study. They tracked down a third of them who agreed to be interviewed every decade about their life. Those interviews produced an amazing finding—one that's important for us.

It turned out that the four-year-olds who were able to hold off the longest turned into teenagers who outperformed their peers in many ways. Here's how author Charles Duhigg described what Mischel learned:

> They discovered that the four-year-olds who could delay grati-
> fication the longest ended up with the best grades and with SAT

scores 210 points higher, on average, than everyone else. They were more popular and did fewer drugs.

Whether it was causation or correlation, self-discipline is a key skill to develop. Some evidence suggests that people who become wealthy use their self-discipline in some very specific ways.

People Who Become Wealthy Pick Their Hard

Tom Corley was only nine when a fire destroyed his father's business and the family's wealth. Growing up poor made him want to understand what it took to become wealthy. He decided to accomplish that by studying the difference between how people with money spent their time and how poor people spent their time. His basic idea was that the little choices we make every day with our habits accumulate to make us wealthy, or not.

Corley spent 5 years studying the daily behavior of 233 people with at least $160K income and net worth above $3 million. He also studied 128 people who made less than $35K and had less than $5K in liquid assets. He found that there was a huge difference between the two groups and put his findings in the book: *Rich Habits: The Daily Success Habits of Wealthy Individuals*. This is not science, like Walter Mischel's research, but it does give us some helpful insights into what it takes to become wealthy.

Corley says he's identified over 300 differences between people who become wealthy and people who don't. You can find selections from his work all over the web, but they all boil down to choices. Here are the ones that seem most important to me.

Wealthy people avoid some things, no matter how much they might like them. They avoid junk food, for example. Poor people are more than three times as likely to eat 300 junk food calories a day. Wealthy people don't watch much TV. Corley says that two-thirds of them watch less than an hour a day. Fewer than a quarter of poor people say that. For wealthy people, picking their hard means avoiding distractions that slow goal achievement.

Wealthy people choose to do things that help them achieve their goals, even if those things aren't "fun." That takes self-discipline.

How to Build Your Self-Discipline

If you want to act like people who earn wealth, you'll need willpower and self-discipline to pick your hard, especially when you know you need to do something hard today to build wealth tomorrow. If you're not yet a very self-disciplined person, don't worry; self-discipline is like a muscle, so you can develop it.

You can build up your willpower the way you build up a physical muscle. Here's some advice on how to do that from Dr. Heidi Grant Halvorson, Associate Director of the Motivation Science Center at Columbia University:

> Before taking on a goal that requires lots of willpower (e.g., quitting smoking, radically changing your diet), start by strengthening your muscle with regular, less strenuous workouts. Add a few willpower challenges to your day (e.g., making your bed, sitting up straight, taking the stairs instead of the elevator) and build from there.

You develop the ability to make wise choices by making wise choices, both big and small. But your willpower muscle can get tired, just like a physical muscle. Most people have more willpower first thing in the morning, before they've used their willpower very much. Try to schedule tasks that require self-discipline early in the day. No matter how much you develop your willpower muscle, sometimes you'll use it to the limit. When that happens, give yourself a recovery break before tackling a tough task or making a hard choice. Do something that lifts your spirit to recover more rapidly.

It's not failure; it's feedback.

Build systems that are biased toward the wise choices and lessen the temptations for poor choices. Greg McKeown's powerful book, *Essentialism,* aims to help you focus on the few things that have a disproportionately powerful and positive effect.

You've heard of the domino effect. Many of us think a one-inch domino can knock over another one-inch domino which can knock over another one-inch domino. Actually, the truth is far more powerful. A one-inch domino can knock over a domino 50% taller, which can knock over a domino more than twice the first one, which can knock over one three times the first, which can knock over one five inches tall. *One Thing: The Surprising Truth behind Extraordinary Results* by Gary Keller reveals this fact and scores of other powerful ideas.

You want to use your willpower muscle for important things, but don't squander it. Here are some ways to save your willpower strength for the times when you really need it.

Avoid temptation. This is so simple that it's easy to forget. If you don't want to eat ice cream, don't buy any. If you decide that you shouldn't watch TV and you don't want to make that decision repeatedly, get rid of your TV, or buy a device to limit television time.

Make it harder to do the wrong thing. This is a variation on the "avoid temptation" idea. You can put a lock on the fridge so you can't just open the door, reach in, and grab that pint of vanilla. Put a sign on the fridge door that says: "Do you want ice cream or do you want to be wealthy?"

Develop habits that make wise choices automatic. Habits are autopilot for your brain. They help you make wise choices without having to do the heavy lifting of making a decision every time. In 1877, psychologist William James wrote a short treatise on "Habit." He suggests that you should start only one new habit at a time and make establishing it a big deal. Never "suffer an exception" until the habit is working and you don't need to think about it anymore.

Remember your "Why." Asking yourself questions like "Why should I do this?" or "What can I do now that will help me become wealthy?" connects the hard choice you're confronting with the bigger picture. Let's say it's the end of a tough day. Dinner is done and you're sitting in your favorite chair. You face a choice. The TV remote and a book about success principles are both in easy reach. Asking yourself "What's the best thing for me to do right now?" can help you pass up that popular show and read that book.

Building your self-discipline is simply developing skills that help you behave like people who become wealthy: habitually doing better things that will bring long-term gain. Wouldn't it be great if you could get lucky, too?

What about luck?

We know the basics of luck. A lucky event is something that's random and unpredictable and has an important impact. Everyone gets both good and bad luck. Motivational speakers contend that our success depends on how we respond to whatever luck we get.

You might think that breaking your arm is bad luck. Well, it means you're not going to be pitching tomorrow, but maybe you'll reorient your life and your sport because of the broken arm. Maybe you'll meet somebody in rehab. Maybe you'll drive more carefully. The fact that something happened is not automatically good or bad, but how you deal with it can make a difference. Pity parties don't advance your goal. The impact of a luck event depends a lot on what you do about things that you control, and a lot of that depends on your attitude. How you respond determines part of your legacy.

There's a popular saying, "Adversity builds character." That may be true, but your legacy is tied to a more important truth: "Adversity reveals character." When things are going well, it's easy to be gracious and treat people well, but what about when things go bad? I've worked with Betty and Paul's children in some very tough times, and they've always been gracious and poised and treated others with respect and dignity. That's part of their legacy.

Adversity isn't the only thing that reveals character; success does, too. We've all known wealthy people who act like they're better than other people. That's a danger you face if you build wealth. It's easy to start thinking of yourself as better than other people. That's why I admire people like Paul and Betty. They became wealthy, but their wealth did not define them. They retained their values and continued to treat others well and taught their children to do the same.

Good luck and bad luck will both challenge you, but I think most of us prefer good luck. We've all known some people who seem to be lucky in everything they do and other people whose lives seem like a succession of disasters. Could it be that the "lucky" ones do things that the "unlucky" ones don't do? Dr. Richard Wiseman, a psychologist, invested a decade researching that question.

Dr. Wiseman is a professor in the Public Understanding of Psychology at the University of Hertfordshire. He advertised in various places, inviting people who considered themselves especially lucky or unlucky to contact him. He interviewed them and asked them to complete questionnaires and psychological assessments. Here's what he found:

> The findings have revealed that luck is not a magical ability or the result of random chance. Nor are people born lucky or unlucky. Instead, although lucky and unlucky people have almost no insight into the real causes of their good and bad luck, *their thoughts and behavior are responsible for much of their fortune.*

Dr. Wiseman put his findings into a book, *The Luck Factor.* The book has been published with several subtitles since it came out in 2003. The one I liked best was "The Scientific Study of the Lucky Mind." The book inspired me to do some research of my own.

Over the last generation I've had substantial conversations with hundreds of millionaires, not all of whom became brokerage clients. I sought to learn what differentiated the investors with good results from the ones with great excuses. My summary, or "principles of wise/lucky thinking," are based on Wiseman's book and my own research.

To win the game, you must be in the game. Many people sit in the stands, while relatively few suit up and get into the competition. So stay involved, meet people, and get out more.

The people whom Wiseman called "lucky," I call "wise." They resisted impulsive actions and avoided foolish risks. Instead, they were more likely to ask their family and friends for perceptions, counsel, and connections; and they were more likely to heed the counsel. Fools ignored counsel or did not seek any seasoned advice and plunged ahead.

Try things. Reflect on what happens. When you move a half-step closer to your goal, keep moving. Wealth building is a long game.

Train yourself to find something good in every situation. Maybe the only good is that you learn that "It hurts like hell to do this, and I'm not going to do that anymore." See? You just got smarter.

Persistence pays. Winners know failure is a way station on the path to success. Quitters stop before they win. I love the story that inspirational speaker Les Brown tells about playing a game with his son. The father won again and again. Finally, Les started to put the game away, but his son wouldn't let him. "No," he said. "It's not over till I win."

Wealthy Acting

F. Scott Fitzgerald wrote that "the rich are different from you and me." He was right and he was wrong. He was right that they have more wealth, but he was wrong to think that that wealth was beyond the reach of most people, people like you and me. Affluent people think and act differently from people who never earn wealth, but you can learn to do what the rich do.

In the next chapter, we'll talk about another cluster of behaviors that will increase the odds that you'll become wealthy. That cluster is called "emotional intelligence."

Emotional Intelligence

"We're all perfectly imperfect."
~ Mindy Bortness

"The warm, fuzzy stuff is hard."
~ Guy Kawasaki

"It is much easier to take men as they are than
to make them as they should be."
~ Marshal de Saxe

People were staring at me because I was crying, right there in the cereal aisle in our luxury supermarket. A week earlier I'd been full of myself and proud of my career at a big, important bank. Now I was crying because I got fired, bawling because I hadn't seen it coming. Sandy was there comforting me, but my ego was shattered and I thought my life was, too. I was the victim of emotional stupidity. Let's go back a little so you get the whole story.

After I got my MBA, I was hired by world's largest bank and inducted into an intense boot camp to become a commercial loan officer. Everyone around me had an MBA from a top tier school; think Stanford or Harvard. Not me. I was hired because someone in the program thought I was really smart. I thought I was special. I was 23 years old. How dumb could someone be? Read on.

In one sense, I did very well. I made my numbers. I earned good raises and promotions and wound up in an extremely prestigious branch. A year into that assignment, I had done 40% more business than my predecessor, my portfolio substantially exceeded the bank's profitability goals, and I had won a statewide contest for opening new accounts. So I thought I was God's gift to banking . . . but I was clueless.

I had so little poise, so little emotional intelligence, that sometimes I didn't know and other times I didn't care how others perceived me. I was clumsy, rude, and arrogant, and I'm ashamed to say I thought I was more important than other people. I was building up a huge amount of anger and resentment all around me, but my delusion was that I was doing great.

One evening at about 6:30, I called the president of one of our client companies at home and said, "I'm calling about the interest payment on your company's line of credit, which was due last week and hasn't come in." Well, naturally, he got angry.

"What? You're calling me at my home because of a clerical error?"

"Well, sir, I'm still working, and I'm finishing up things here, and I just noticed this." I thought he'd be impressed that I was working late. Nope. I should have called their office during the work day and talked to accounts payable. Calling the CEO at home was criminally dumb. It was also the final straw, the one that got me fired.

This chapter is about emotional intelligence (EI). You'll learn what it is and why it's important when you're investing in apartments. You'll learn some common situations where a lack of emotional intelligence can get you in trouble, and you'll read how things look when they go right. You'll also discover the most important way to make sure that emotions don't derail your wealth train.

What Is Emotional Intelligence?

You've probably heard about emotional intelligence, thanks to Daniel Goleman. After he got his PhD in psychology from Harvard, he wound up writing for *Psychology Today* and then the *New York Times*. That's when Goleman read an academic paper by two other psychologists, John Mayer and Peter Salovey, that outlined the basics of what they called "emotional intelligence." His 1995 best-selling book titled, appropriately enough, *Emotional Intelligence* popularized the phrase.

Goleman breaks down emotional intelligence into five categories that include a total of 25 competencies. The details are in Goleman's books. *The Oxford Dictionary* defines emotional intelligence this way:

> The capacity of individuals to recognize their own, and other people's emotions, to discriminate between different feelings and label them appropriately, to use emotional information to guide thinking and behavior, and to manage and/or adjust emotions to adapt environments or achieve one's goal(s).

That's better, but it's still more academic than I like. Luckily, Kimberlyn Leary, Julianna Pillemer, and Michael Wheeler came up with a more practical definition in their *Harvard Business Review* article, "Negotiating with Emotion." Specifically, emotionally intelligent people have the capacity to:

- identify the emotions they and others are experiencing;
- understand how those emotions affect their thinking;
- use that knowledge to achieve better outcomes;
- productively manage emotions, tempering or intensifying them for whatever purpose.

Look at those four items and think of the 23-year-old me. I sure wasn't any good at identifying the emotions that other people were experiencing. I had no idea how those emotions affected their thinking or my own. And I definitely wasn't able to productively manage emotions or achieve better outcomes. Since I was too socially clumsy, it's no surprise that I was fired.

Actually, emotional intelligence goes by a lot of names. It's what we mean when we talk about "soft skills" or "people skills" or when we say that someone is "good with people." Your grandma might have used the term "character" or "poise." Paul and Betty's adult children exhibit poise. I'm still striving to improve; poise helps every broker and every investor.

Why Is Emotional Intelligence Important for Apartment Investors?

Investing in apartments is a high-stakes activity. There's a lot of money on the line. You'll read and hear advice that to succeed you should be perfectly rational, the kind of people that Nobel Laureate economist Richard Thaler calls *econs*. They live in economics textbooks where they're always totally rational and seeking to maximize financial gain. I think of them as Mr. Spock from *Star Trek*, but with a profit motive. But guess what? They don't exist in real life.

In real life, we're messy, emotional creatures. Nobel Laureate Daniel Kahneman described how emotions affect our decision making in his book *Thinking, Fast and Slow*. You will only build legacy wealth by investing in apartments if you learn that everyone brings emotions to their decision making and to the negotiating table. The result is that smart people, including you and me, often do dumb things.

The best investors have and cultivate emotional intelligence. Patient, tactful people close great deals even with principals who act like jerks. Other people go away from jerks feeling self-justified but without a deal. You don't want to miss superior opportunities just because the other person is difficult. Wise buyers can capture the good property and ignore sellers' folly or greed.

Savvy investors can close even though the other side is silly, mentally limited, bigoted, misinformed, or of the other political tribe. You may not invite the other side to vacation with you, but you can close with them and win. Sure, they may do things that irritate you, and their quirks are different from my quirks or yours; but that doesn't mean you can't conclude a transaction that benefits you.

When push comes to shove, all personal choices, including income property choices, involve human reactions in situations with incomplete and conflicting information. You'll almost always have more emotion inside you than you want others to know about. Both sides have some anxiety, confusion, doubt, fear, greed, hope, and regret.

How Things Go Wrong

Things go wrong because people are people. That sounds simple, maybe even simplistic, but it's important to remember. We will do some things that are not in our best interest because people aren't perfect. Emotional intelligence involves being aware of your emotions and choosing your responses. Here are four common situations my clients and I experience regularly.

1. **All-or-nothing thinking**

   There are no perfect properties. Every property you will ever consider buying has something wrong with it. Smart investors look for properties with the right things wrong with them, fixable problems. The assets become more valuable after the problems are solved. Some people don't get that. They lose sight of the big picture and the upside of the property and get stuck on fixable flaws.

   For example, some investors inspect a property and learn that it's got 20-year-old carpet or a paint color they don't like. They focus on fixable trivia and they walk away from the deal. Perhaps the seller is a jerk or the current management firm is rude to tenants. Flawed thinking would be "I don't want to reward bad management" or "the property can never get better." More mature analysis recognizes that considerate, effective management could obtain better results with little extra cost.

The way to defeat all-or-nothing thinking is to constantly ask two questions. First ask, "What would it take to fix those flaws?" Then ask, "What will that do to the value of the property?" Those two questions can facilitate your wise judgment about whether to invest in a particular property.

2. **Falling prey to common decision biases**
Shortcuts are often helpful, but sometimes what seems like a shortcut does not work. Mental shortcuts are called *decision biases* or *cognitive biases*. A common one during the selling process is the endowment effect. Here's the description from Richard Thaler, who coined the term:

> The tendency for people to demand much more to give up an object than they would be willing to pay to acquire it.

Now when you catch yourself valuing your property more than the amount that others come up with through rational, number-crunching analysis, you can think to yourself, "Maybe I'm guilty of the endowment effect." When that happens, take a step back and reassess.

Another common decision bias is information bias. I see this with clients who never close. They keep asking for more and more information and analysis, even though whatever they find will not affect the decision. When you catch yourself asking for more and more information or analysis, ask yourself: "Will the information change my decision, or am I just avoiding a decision?"

3. **Living in the past instead of learning from it**
Most people have common decision biases—thinking shortcuts. We also have our own personal decision biases, shortcuts we use because

of a "lesson" that we've learned from specific situations. Negative outcomes affect us more than positive ones, so this kind of decision bias is likely to hold you back from making a decision you should make. Here's an example.

I recently worked with a client who has a decades-long track record of successful business and investing decisions. Recently, though, a broker talked him into decisions that really weren't in his best interest. He realized that he was too polite to be assertive, but, at least for now, he doesn't trust his instincts and the vast majority of his experience. Instead of analyzing the situation in front of him and then deciding, he's overcautious, nervous, and hesitant.

In my experience, people act that way when a transaction or two have gone badly and they feel like they've been "talked into" a bad decision. They may be angry because they felt like they were manipulated. That powerful, negative emotion holds them back and keeps them from making rational, timely decisions.

This is different from information bias because it's tied to a single event or transaction, or possibly two, and it's emotionally charged. You need to step back and review the current situation and compare it with the previous one. Compare the timing, the people involved, and the numbers. Often, that rational analysis will drain away the emotion and let you see both situations clearly. A great broker may articulate the differences and help you focus on making a wise choice now.

4. **Blowing a crucial conversation, maybe trying to teach the other person a lesson**
Earlier in this chapter, you read, "Patient, tactful people close great deals even with principals who act like jerks." That's true, but it isn't easy. Getting angry is something we human beings do all the time, even when it isn't good for us. Something happens that trips our anger switch, and suddenly we're behaving like a jerk.

Maybe you've been cut off in traffic by another driver and moved right up on the other car's bumper because you were going to "show them." Have you ever had an argument with a friend or your spouse and afterward wondered why you said all those hurtful things? Those situations are so common that Daniel Goleman created a term for them: *amygdala hijack*.

The amygdala is a small, walnut-shaped part of your brain. It triggers the responses that helped keep our ancestors safe from saber-toothed tigers. When it perceives a threat, the amygdala sends signals to prepare the body for fight or flight. Adrenaline gets dumped into the bloodstream, and blood is redirected from the brain to major muscle groups in the arms and legs. That makes you better able to run or fight, but far less able to think clearly. We call it an amygdala hijack when the response is out of proportion to the actual threat.

When that happens to you, you can't think clearly. In other words, you become dumber when you need to be at your mental peak. You're likely to shift into the modern version of fight-or-flight mode and decide to teach the other person a lesson. That never helps. I work as a mediator from time to time. Skilled mediators know:

> You can have your say or you can have your way, but you can't have both.

Having your way means coming out of the negotiations with a good deal, one that helps you to build wealth. You can vent your spleen or give the other party a piece of your mind, but it won't help you close a deal. If you're building wealth by investing in apartments, you will encounter situations and people that might hijack your amygdala. You need to know how to prevent it and what to do when it starts to happen.

For example, you may encounter someone who consistently acts like a rectum. You'll be tempted to respond in kind, even though you know it's a bad idea. Good preparation for a negotiation will help you keep from having your amygdala hijacked. Preparation always includes quantitative issues and negotiating points. It should also include planning how you will respond to the other side's provocative behavior. Role playing before difficult conversations can help.

If you anticipate the other side's possible behavior, you can prepare for it. You'll also be less likely to be hooked emotionally. Good preparation dampens many of the emotional reactions you might have responding to provocative behavior. That can help you keep your cool and restrict your strong emotion. But how *should* you respond?

A few years ago, I was representing two of Paul and Betty's adult children in a negotiation with a man who routinely acted selfishly. We had been negotiating with this fellow for weeks, and it was beginning to look like we would never come to a good conclusion. I could feel myself getting angrier and starting to pay more attention to my emotions than I was to the negotiation, classic signs of an amygdala hijack.

Part of Betty and Paul's legacy was showing their children how to deal with difficult people and situations. I've represented several of them and they all have poise, a kind of "grace under pressure." On that day, I was blessed to have one of their daughters at the table with me.

She didn't indulge in aggressive emotions. Instead, very quietly, she looked the man across the table in the eye and said, "Look. You want to sell your building. We want to buy your building. Let's get it done. This can be good for both of us." We did the deal. Her response is a perfect example of the principle of dealing with provocative emotion:

Fight fire with water, not more fire.

You may not have the kind of poise my client has. I'm striving for that skill. Here are some things you can do to help situations come out right, even when emotions run high. Spend some time reflecting on your personal triggers. When you know them, you will recognize them, and you'll be more likely to keep your amygdala from being hijacked. Remember your mother's advice to "count to ten before you speak." It's still good advice; the counting will access the rational parts of your brain and help you calm down.

When you think your amygdala is being hijacked, take a break. Getting away from the situation, drinking some water (not coffee), thinking calm and pleasant thoughts, and having a quiet conversation with your spouse or broker will help you regain your emotional balance.

Obviously, staying in control makes it more likely that things will turn out well for you, but consider something else, too. Your legacy is wrapped up in how people remember you. How do you suppose people in that room remember and think about that selfish fellow? Will they want to do business with him in the future? What will they say about him to other people?

Now think about my client. How will the people in that room remember her? How will they describe her to others? When they tell the story of that day, who will be the hero? Will it be the selfish fink or the poised woman with the gentle strength who ensured the deal was done?

Thankfully I have more emotional intelligence now than I had back in my bank days, but I can still do much better. I look for simple things that will help me act the way I want to act and be remembered.

5. Confusing being right with capturing an opportunity

Since the first edition was published I served two smart investors who fumbled superior opportunities. In both cases the buyer focused on property imperfections, (there are always imperfections), and exaggerated what it would take to bring apartments to acceptable standard. In both cases the buyer picked an irrelevant measure. One lady compared working-class apartments to her million-dollar home. Although she wasn't stupid, she negotiated as if the minimum standard for working-class apartments was comparable to her home. Her temporary blindness meant that she assumed repairs would cost triple what was needed. She didn't realize that her standard for her home was beyond what renters could afford.

It was as if a Mercedes' owner couldn't imagine that most people couldn't afford a new Lexus. Her condo's tenants had twice the income of the renters of the apartments she had in escrow. She had trouble understanding what the apartment renters could afford and expected a kitchen like the one next door, not like her luxury level. That landlady walked away from the best deal that we had found in months. Another buyer bought the building, rehabbed it, spending one-third of what she considered minimum necessary. The new owners are thrilled with the investment, its appreciation; the residents are well pleased. It has been a year and the landlady has not bought any other rentals.

Another client put an older building under contract; one built on a raised foundation instead of slab on grade. This analytical buyer ignored what would be needed to bring the assets in line with similar assets. Instead he focused on what it would cost to bring it to current building code. He asked for concessions more than six times what I suggested was appropriate. The escrow was canceled. Other buyers eagerly acquired what he rejected. The ultimate buyers were fully satisfied with an effective solution..

Both buyers were positive they knew best. Anybody who had another idea was foolish or delusional. My understanding is different. People drive used cars and live in used homes. Successful investors seek a profitable investment, not necessarily a perfect investment. Few successful landlords seek the local historical society's restoration of the year award.

One Important Way to Make Emotional Intelligence Work for You

Remember the Golden Rule: Treat others the way you want to be treated. Make it easy for the other side to win while attending to your own interest, and you'll enjoy many transactions where both sides win. Negotiators who believe they are smarter than or tougher than or sneakier than the other side, are sometimes right but often don't close. Ronald Reagan quoted the

Russian proverb: "trust but verify." The tactic reduced the risk of global destruction; it also works in investment real estate.

Developing your emotional intelligence will help. Be aware of how feelings affect everyone's choices and reactions. Learn to choose what to initiate, when to respond, and how to respond in ways that are true and useful and a blessing. We all can learn to do better.

My client's emotional intelligence saved a whole room full of people from themselves. As a broker, I often do that for my clients. Part of my job is to keep you away from the emotional and mental cliffs and cul-de-sacs that might distract you from the worthwhile goal of legacy wealth.

This book is about legacy. Our media do not value courtesy or poise. When you aspire to and model emotional intelligence, your choices will impact those near you. Some people took coed dance as adolescents or typing in school. Many hated such disciplines then, but have been grateful for them in the decades since then. You are in position of impact now. Use your influence for good during your fleeting season of maximum influence.

Think About the Legacy You Want to Leave

I've been to many funerals over the years, and I've noticed that business and investing success only gets a passing mention, if that. Whether it's in the eulogy, the memorial service testimony, or the graveside conversations, when you're gone, people will remember the person you were more than how successful you were.

That's a handy way to sort this out for yourself. How do you want people to remember you? What do you want to be known for?

One fellow I served was a billionaire who could not name his grandkids. Another is a millionaire landscaper who kept his rents at least 25% below market rents. His daughter lives rent free. He mows his parents' yard for free.

Both men succeeded beyond their young dreams, but they sought differing legacies. What legacy do you want? What stories do you want people to tell about you after you're gone?

Let me make this personal. I want to be remembered as a great husband to Sandy, as someone who vigorously tried to treat others the way I want to be treated, as a man who took prudent risks, and as a determined, yet flawed, follower of Jesus who strove to live out his faith. I hope people will remember me as congruent, whether at work, play, home, or worship. Those aspirations govern my key life choices.

As I write this book, Sandy has been battered by the loss of her father, by a foot surgery, and by a host of other large and small issues. To cushion and protect her, I need to set aside some actions and activities I cherish. Day by day, my choices show whether I'm giving up Sandy for my goals or giving up my goals for Sandy. I've not been famous for sacrificial love. There is a cost. Each wise person picks their hard. Now, it's your turn to be honest.

What Do You Want Said at Your Funeral or Memorial Service?

Let me nudge you gently. Take the time to write it out. Go ahead; put a few things on paper. Things that seem super-clear when you think about them may not be so clear when you start to write them down. That's normal. It won't be perfect the first time. Put it away for a day or so. There are host of resources for this exercise. You don't need academic perfection to develop useful insight.

When you review what you've written, you may notice some things you want to change. That's normal, too. Make the changes you want to make before you go on to the next step.

Ready? OK. How would the person you want to be act? If you don't turn those values into behaviors, they're just hope. Here are some examples.

A woman I knew wanted people to think of her as "gracious." She knew that gracious people thanked others. She made a habit of writing three thank-you notes every day.

A man who was a plant manager wanted to be known as "friendly and down-to-earth." He thought that would happen if he had conversations with plant workers every day. When that didn't happen automatically, he decided to walk around the plant three times a day, which gave him opportunities for conversations.

Think about that person you want to be. How would he or she spend time and money? How would he or she act? That's important, but it's only the first part of creating a legacy that you want and will be proud of. The hard part is living it.

We tend to measure our behavior by what we intend to do, not by what we actually do. Do you know about Alfred Nobel's first obituary?

You probably know Alfred Nobel because of the Nobel Prizes. You may also know that he invented dynamite, a detonator, and a blasting cap. He was awarded more than three hundred patents, many of which were for explosives and weapons, and he owned a company that manufactured military weapons. Nobel probably thought he was a good fellow. He went to church and gave to charity. He was kind to the people around him. Then, in 1888, his brother Ludvig died.

A French newspaper mistakenly thought it was Alfred who died and published a long, harsh obituary of Alfred under the headline, "The Merchant of Death is Dead." Alfred knew instantly that if he had died, people would remember him as "the Merchant of Death." He did not want to be remembered that way. He changed many things in his life and business and used his fortune to establish the Nobel Prizes for people who do things that benefit humanity.

Alfred Nobel was lucky. He got to see his obituary while he could still do things differently and change the way he would be remembered. You probably won't have that opportunity, but you can take a hard look at your behavior and judge whether your legacy will be what you want it to be.

Developing your own emotional intelligence will help you become a better investor and a better person. You will also increase the odds of building legacy wealth if you clarify your values and priorities. That's what the next chapter is about.

Understand Your Values and Priorities

"There are no easy answers, there are only intelligent choices."
~ CATERPILLAR TRACTOR AD

"Thinking is the hardest work there is,
which is the probable reason why so few engage in it."
~ HENRY FORD

"Cherish forever what makes you unique,
'cuz you're really a yawn if it goes!"
~ BETTE MIDLER

THE NEXT FEW PAGES MAY BE UNCOMFORTABLE for some readers. Trust me; they'll be worth your time. Some readers might find these ideas more important than the wealth-building pages. One of my smartest and most successful investors recently faced a serious investment challenge because he had not fully reconciled himself as to his goals and priorities.

More than 30 years ago, I did my first values-clarification exercise. I had to choose between various pairs of opposites. The vital choices weren't easy. For example, to rank health and wealth, you could choose being poor and healthy or rich, but sick. Another choice was between being a great spouse and adequate at work or being star at work and being divorced. I knew what was important to me. I wanted to be a good husband. I felt good about my choices.

Then came the killer or verification question: "Does your time show that that's what really matters to you? If you want to be a spectacular husband, are you spending discretionary time with Sandy?" How you use your discretionary time, money, and thoughts reveal your choices.

The sad truth was that although I said that being a terrific husband to Sandy was important to me, my actions revealed that work mattered more. My actions spoke louder than my words. I was embarrassed, and angry, about my inconsistency. For more than a generation since then, I've been laboring to increase consistency between what I say I believe and what I do.

What you do with your time, your talent, and your treasure shows what you truly value and thus what will be the legacy you leave.

It would be nice if there was a "sit on the couch, eat ice cream, gain muscle, and lose weight" diet, but there isn't. There also isn't a perfect property or an investing strategy that's the best choice for everyone. You must pick your hard. There are always trade-offs. When you understand what truly matters to you, it's easier to make wise choices, live a better life, and be a more successful investor. This chapter will help you understand your values and live them out.

If you'll do your own values-clarification exercise, then you'll clarify what matters to you and whether you want to make any adjustments. Many of us shift priorities with passing decades, even when our values remain constant. Next, you'll learn the five common goals for investing in rental property. The goal that fits best now may not be the most appropriate goal in your next generation. We'll explore five important trade-offs in apartment investing, and you'll discover why investing in a zip code where you don't want to live may be the best way to build your wealth and create your legacy.

Each person, each investor, is unique. Some of us like chocolate ice cream, others like vanilla, and still others don't like ice cream at all. Knowing what's important to you simplifies decision making. When my clients explain what's important to them, our chances of success increase because my team can systematically search for and help them capture their best opportunity.

I've worked with many people over the years. The very best investors shared two things. They knew what they wanted from their investments and they were clear about who they were. Many investing books encourage you to articulate your investment goals, and that's important; but it's equally important to know who you want to be and the legacy you want to leave.

Are You Acting Like the Person You Want to Be?

Don't be too quick to answer this. Look at your calendar and your checkbook. How are you spending your time and your money? If my experience is any guide, you might discover that your actions show different priorities than your words.

Over the years since that first values-clarification exercise, I've reviewed my behavior against my ideal periodically. Each time I recognize gaps between reality and my aspirations. Humility means understanding the truth about yourself.

If you're willing, consider one more step. Ask people who know you well and care enough to tell you the truth about how you act. Remember that how you act will determine your legacy, so hear what they say. Don't be surprised if you don't like everything you hear. Criticism is a gift; often it can be helpful. Recognize that truth is your friend, even when you don't like the truth. You can't change the past, so if you want to lead a life worth imitating, your future behavior is the key.

This is one of those "good news, bad news" situations. The good news is that identifying the legacy you want to leave, what you want to be known for, makes it more likely that it will happen. The other news is that you will work on your legacy for the rest of your life. One way that you will work to leave the legacy you choose is by choosing your goals wisely; and to do that, you should know the options.

Five Goals for Income Property Investing

Every investor has a unique situation and investing goals, but those goals tend to fall into one of the following five categories. As you read the descriptions, think about your life, goals, and values. Try to identify which one is best for you right now.

1. **Build wealth**
    Many of my clients aim to build wealth, and they work to speed up the process. Like Paul and Betty, they may manage their properties and/or do some of the maintenance themselves.

2. **Maximize cash flow**
    This goal is often for people who are at least retirement age and content with their net worth. They've built a substantial inheritance, and they've been deferring gratification for a generation or more. The extra cash will enable them to do things they've always wanted to do but put off. Maybe they want to tour in a Class-A motorhome or take luxury cruises. For a generation or more, they have deferred gratification; now they are ready to savor the fruits of their labor.

3. **Steady cash flow with almost no management**
    At "retirement age," many households move equity out of apartments into buildings leased by a national business tenant with bond-rated credit. Single-tenant, triple-net investments are properties where only one

business rents the entire building. That business is so financially strong that their bonds, unsecured debt, are publicly traded on the national stock exchanges. Widows and pension funds invest in the bonds. Real estate investors rent buildings to these corporations. This investment can be good for households who are content with their net worth, those who seek steady, low-risk cash flow for 10–30 years. This investment is not a wealth-building strategy, but an income-harvesting mechanism.

4. **Pride of ownership**
Some investors buy rental properties that show their wealth. These investors don't need more money, but they want the admiration and recognition. In effect, the purchase testifies that they don't need or care about cash flow; it symbolizes their success.

5. **Fallback property**
"Fallback Property" is tangible insurance. You could live there yourself if your circumstances crumble, or you could rent to your sister at a discount if she separated from her husband. A fallback property will be in a nice neighborhood with educated, well-socialized neighbors, but its cash flow will be lower than ordinary neighborhoods (look at the trade-offs in a few paragraphs). Don't expect to maximize cash flow or wealth.

Many investors begin with one of these five categories. Wisdom means knowing your objective and the best way to accomplish it. For example, if you want to be seen as wise, then choose wisely. If your goal is to build legacy wealth, you'll benefit from this book's tools and techniques, beginning with an overview of the key trade-offs in apartment investing.

Five Important Trade-offs in Apartment Investing

There are no perfect properties, so you must assess the trade-offs in every opportunity. Here are common trade-offs I've identified in apartment investing:

1. **Easy management and superior condition versus creating extra value**
   Properties that are easy to manage usually have good tenants, and they're in good neighborhoods. You pay a premium to own them, and there's little you can do to improve them. In contrast, when a property has "the right things wrong with it," you can increase the property's value by fixing the problems. The key is to identify the problems that cost little but boost the value the most, (i.e., the right things wrong with it).

2. **Prestigious neighborhood versus higher cash flow**
   "Location, location, location" may be how you decide where you live. The fact that your tenants' kids attend the best school district does not guarantee that your equity will grow at even an average pace. Prestigious neighborhoods command a higher price, but areas with lower credit scores and lower education levels sell for less. In San Diego County, the zip codes with advanced-degree tenants sell for three to four times the zip codes where high school dropouts live. The working-class zip codes often generate more wealth for rental owners.

3. **Maximum wealth or keeping your trophy properties**
   Maybe you already own rentals, so you are an apprentice or beyond. Or maybe you're getting started. Perhaps one day you'll have a property that is special, one where the real estate means more to you than its return justifies. To build the wealth you aspire to, you will decide whether to keep this small trophy with its modest cash flow or trade it in.

   There are at least two right answers. Some will cherish the property like their first trophy or maybe their kid's teddy bear. It's fine to value comfort and memory as more important than maximizing wealth or more tax shelter or more trips or a bigger donation. Great, understood.

   Another correct answer is that every investment is a tool, not a child. If I can trade that equity for a bigger goal or a worthier investment vehicle, I'll do it. In a decade, everything I own will be older;

I'd rather have more tax shelter now and greater capacity to help my family or travel in a decade. Sure, I traded in my first car for the newer one. That choice is also a right answer.

One of my most powerful clients just had a terrible choice to make because he had not reconciled this issue. He was deeply committed to an ambitious financial goal. A once-in–a-generation opportunity came along. Our team worked with him to help clarify his options and, in the end, he decided to keep his small trophy instead of selling it to capture his best wealth-building option. Our team understands and respects his choice, and we're glad to serve him. His actions, not his words, showed what really matters to him.

4. **Property management versus full control for chance of higher cash flow**
    Some people prefer not to ever get involved with the property or tenants. Property management firms will screen tenants, handle repairs, do the accounting and more . . . for a fee. There's a price for that, because the more you do yourself, the more you reap the benefits of lower operating costs. At the same time, you must consider the opportunity cost of your time. Can you earn more by doing something else, or by doing the work yourself and not hiring it out?

5. **Maximum leverage versus lowest possible price**
    When I was a kid, I rode bike with no gears, a one-speed bike. Now I ride an 18-gear bike, magnifying my efficiency and speed. It is easier to go uphill in a lower gear and faster in a higher gear.
    Leverage is a force multiplier not just in bikes and cars, but in finance. Borrowing money gives you leverage. It is possible to borrow two or three times as much as your down payment. That can mean that your profit could be multiplied because of the leverage, the force multiplier.

Maximizing debt can buy more property, which is great in a rising market. Leverage is a double-edged sword, because your mortgage payment and financial risk are higher. Leverage enables you to control two to four times as much property with a loan than with all cash.

The other extreme is no-debt, all-cash purchases. Some seller might discount 3%, maybe even 5%, for fast close, say closing three weeks instead of two months. Institutional lenders will take 6 to 10 weeks to fund an apartment loan. Buyers with loads of cash or who will pay for "hard money" loans can sometimes buy with these discounts or capture a highly desirable asset faster than other investors who need conventional bank financing.

So far, we've listed things you need to know to improve your odds of successfully investing in apartments. This section has been more about thinking than about action. In the next section you'll learn about real-life steps you should take to prepare to invest profitably.

Prepare to Invest Profitably in Apartments

This section's three chapters outline specific things to do before you begin buying, improving, and selling apartment buildings.

The first chapter is **Team Up with a Great Broker**. You'll learn how to choose the best broker for you. A great broker has deep knowledge of the market, of course, but he or she will also understand that your broker's job is to help you make wise decisions. An expert broker is your guide, your protector, and your advisor about relative value, pointing out arbitrage opportunities. Your broker can be a coach, maybe even an accountability partner.

Strong processes, or systems, improve communication and accountability, help assure that everything gets done, and focus your attention on the important things. The chapter, **Make Sure You Have a System That Will Work for You Every Time,** will help you and your broker develop a system you will use repeatedly as you build your legacy wealth.

Many smart investors had the resources to build their legacy wealth, but they failed because they didn't understand some truths. The chapter on **Apartment Investing Realities** explains many of those truths.

Team Up with a Great Broker

"Each honest calling, each walk of life, has its own elite, its own
aristocracy, based on excellence of performance."
~ JAMES BRYANT CONANT

"Mediocrity knows nothing higher than itself,
but talent instantly recognizes genius."
~ ARTHUR CONAN DOYLE

"An expert is someone who knows some of the worst mistakes
that can be made in his subject and how to avoid them."
~ WERNER HEISENBERG

I MET "MARK AND SHARON" IN THEIR 40s. It was the second marriage for both of them. When they got married, they bought a new home
together and rented out the house and condo they had lived in before.
They were thinking of buying another rental house when a trusted friend
referred them to me.

Over the past seven years, we traded the two rentals into some apartments, cleaned them up, painted them up, fixed them up, and sold them for a profit. They doubled their equity in each investment within three years. Today, Sharon and Mark own 90 units and we expect they'll buy more. They are among my great clients.

Mark and Sharon know what they want in life and in investment real estate. They invest the time and attention to build their legacy wealth. They also have a bias for action. They do their homework, and when it's time to make a decision, they make it. When it's time to close, they pull the trigger. They listen to my advice, and they ask important questions. When they come across a possible opportunity on their own, they call me to discuss it. We make a great team.

In this chapter, you'll learn why teaming up with a great broker can dramatically enhance your likelihood of success, what to look for in a broker who will be a great teammate, and how to identify the right broker for you. You'll also learn how to be a great client and teammate, because you're more likely to win if you play investment real estate as a team sport.

You'll read some examples of how superior brokers create far more value than their fee. The examples are real. The stories are not so you'll be impressed with our team, but to impress upon you how the master craftsman far exceeds the journeyman.

Why a Broker-Client Team Is More Likely to Win

Some infomercials promise you quick and easy wealth if you pay for their system and use their "secrets." Like most things that seem too good to be true, they are. There are no secrets, and there are no shortcuts. Success in any field requires work. One thing you should work at is choosing a broker who will be an excellent partner for you.

Some infomercials claim you can beat the professional in their own backyard. Maybe you can, but it's unlikely for a single transaction and almost impossible over the course of many. An expert broker brings mastery of technique and market knowledge that takes years of work and dedication. Will you gamble your fortune and future that you can beat the best at their own game on their home court?

Finding the right broker for you, like finding the right investment, takes work. Too many investors settle for mediocrity when excellence is available. Decline the broker who is a poor fit for you or who is not a great broker. Invest your time and energy to find an excellent broker who *is* a good fit for you. Read on to learn how to find that winning broker.

One terrific broker is better than many adequate ones.

Some people think they are better served by working with many agents. That may make sense in some markets where brokers don't cooperate very much. Those markets have lower volume because fewer people know about available options. East Coast and Mid-Atlantic markets tend to have low volume and limited brokerage cooperation. If you invest in one of those markets, you may be wise to talk with each of the major players rather than be loyal to one, because no broker will be aware of even 90% of the available properties.

Generally, in most markets, I believe you are better served to hire the best broker to represent you and work only with that broker. If you are loyal and devoted, you can expect those same qualities of your broker. Splitting your attention among multiple brokers will decrease any single broker's incentive to work with you.

Work with the best

Mediocre brokerage is easy to obtain, and you should reject it. A *good* broker is not good enough for someone who wants to build legacy wealth. Part of your legacy should be seeking and finding excellent value in services as well as in buildings. A *great* broker helps ordinary investors obtain sustained, superior success.

A superb broker knows the craft of investment real estate. Every broker must meet state licensing requirements that test their knowledge of the business and the relevant laws. After that, brokerage is an apprentice trade. Most commercial agents begin by helping a senior broker who, in turn, helps them learn the ins and outs of the business. Knowledgeable coaches and expert observers say most agents need 7 to 10 years to grow from novice to master. People, whether brokers or investors, enter the field as novices, start as apprentices, and develop the skills of a journeyman; and a few advance to master craftsman.

Champion brokers know the market in intricate detail. They have been involved with many buildings and know who other brokers and owners are and how they do business. They can advise on arbitrage. A winning broker will be able to say "In this zip code, that price is a bargain. If it was two zip codes over, it wouldn't be a bargain. But in that zip code, it's a $20 bill on sale for $17!"

Novice investors often imagine a competition between buyer and seller. In slow markets, that can be true. In more intense markets, the real contest is between many motivated buyers who are competing to capture the few worthwhile market opportunities. On the other hand, during a recession, in most markets the sellers might be competing with desperate sellers to obtain the cash of few brave buyers. A star broker provides wisdom about market momentum. That sage counsel often makes the difference between a closed transaction and a failed effort.

A fantastic broker can give you an accurate idea of what your property is worth and how hard or easy it will be to sell. He or she will tell you, "Here are the challenges that we're going to face in selling this particular property." Or "This property's going to be easy. It's the best thing since sliced bread."

Knowing the market means more than knowing the geography and the buildings. The best brokers know the other top brokers. Those great brokers will also know the best inspectors, mortgage brokers, and property management companies, too, like a professional coach who knows the tendencies and skills of opponents.

A great broker can help you become more successful. But no matter how good your broker is, he or she can't do it alone.

There are no generic "best properties" that are a good buy for everyone. Your broker can't find the properties that are good investments for you right now, unless you know and share what's important to you, your values, and your investment goals. Your broker can use market knowledge and professional tools to identify properties that may be a good fit for you, but you must analyze the opportunities and then decide whether to make an offer or not.

Here's how that works with Mark and Sharon. Some of the things they do are unique to them, but the basic outline is the same for most of my successful clients.

They are clear about their wealth-building goals and about the kinds of properties that will help them reach those goals. They review their holdings regularly and decide when it's time to redeploy some of their capital by moving up from something they own. Then I identify some possibilities.

Mark looks at many possibilities by driving around and checking out the properties and the neighborhoods. Usually he finds several that are pretty good. Then Sharon reviews what Mark and I have suggested. Her veto power often eliminates one or more. This division of labor is unique to Mark and Sharon. But all the great investors review the many possibilities to identify the best properties for them right then.

We write offers on the best prospects. Usually, we wind up closing on one of them. All those pieces are important, both the knowing and the doing.

After they acquire a property, Mark and Sharon improve it. We discuss how to maximize the property's value and how to sequence the improvements. Sometimes they decide to sell the property after we review their holdings and strategy. Other times, another broker brings an offer. That's what happened in what I call "The College Education Sale."

Mark and Sharon had held one property for about two years while they improved it. One day another broker called them and said, "You have a good property. My client would like to buy it for a million bucks." Sharon said, "Thank you very much. That's a nice offer. Please send everything to Terry and he'll be in touch."

I evaluated the property. The higher rents had raised the value, and the market had improved. I believed bank appraisers would value the property for more than a million. In our market, there was big demand for improved assets. In other words, I knew the market would pay above a conventional appraisal. I explained my reasons to Sharon and Mark. They decided to sell their property.

I added slightly more than 10% to the price to provide some negotiating room. We listed it above my expected appraised value and did intense marketing. Our team reached out to thousands of brokers and more than 10,000 property buyers and owners. In effect, I created a bidding war—a war that my clients won. Within 6 weeks, more than 20 different buyer groups had looked at the property. We received 10 as-is/where-is offers and sold the property above the list price. They earned $100K more than the initial offer because our team understood the market and harnessed the power of "supply and demand" of potential investors.

Now, why do I call it "The College Education Sale?" Their daughters will receive partial scholarships because of their grades and test scores. Mark and Sharon netted about $100K more than the unsolicited offer. That extra money would pay for a fine college education after their daughters' scholarships. Actually, though, Sharon and Mark did even better than that because they didn't pay taxes on that extra profit and then pay for college. Instead, they rolled the money over so it kept earning for them. By the time their first daughter goes to college, it may have grown to a quarter of a million dollars.

We have a great partnership because we each bring something to it. I bring deep knowledge of investment real estate and the experience that comes from two decades of success. Mark and Sharon know what's important to them and what they value. I adapt to the way they work as a couple, and they adapt to my process for evaluating investment opportunities. I trust them to make wise decisions, and they trust my professional abilities. When it's time to close, they close.

Mark and Sharon are model clients, and we make a great team. To find and recognize a great partner for that kind of long-term relationship, you must know what to look for.

What a Great Broker Looks Like

The perfect broker does not exist. Neither does the perfect client. Here are my ideas about what you should look for when you set out to find a great broker to work with. The more of these traits you discover, the better will be your chances of safe and profitable investing.

Great brokers deliver great results. Top performers in any field don't outperform their run-of-the-mill colleagues by a whisker, but often by a large margin. Capturing the best deal of the year compared to missing that property can easily exceed a year's income for most investors. Remember "The College Education Story?"

Bear with a few numbers. They are cited not to impress you, but to impress upon you the rarity and importance of excellence.

San Diego County has 15,000+ agents. In the last generation, there have been more than 10,000 apartment building listings. Only 42% of those apartment listings sold during their listing period. My team's success rate is 85%.

Experts specialize. Fewer than 1% of the agents have closed even a tenth as many apartment escrows as my team. You should hire a proven expert in your market. Stated simply, if you need brain surgery, don't use a general practitioner. Expert brokers will help you get into a rising market and rescue your capital during a falling market.

Top-performing brokers do many things differently. Based on client feedback and my experience, here are the top six qualities: client focus— hears you and focuses on maximizing your result; trustworthiness and truthfulness; skilled teacher; shock absorber; achiever of superior results; and understanding of your motivation, your legacy goals.

1. **A great broker puts the client first**

   This should be true for every broker, but unfortunately it isn't. Too many brokers will show you the properties they've listed before they show any other properties because they make more money if you buy a property they've listed. Too many brokers will go silent on an important bit of information (neighborhood risk, potential property problems, better deal listed by a competitor) because your best choice might mean a lower commission for them.

   You must trust your broker's professional knowledge, and you must also trust that your broker will put your interests first. If you ever go to court as a witness, you will swear to tell "the truth, the whole truth, and nothing but the truth." That's the standard you should hold a broker to. If you don't feel a broker will do that for you, find a different broker.

   If you don't trust your broker, then you're wasting everyone's time. When a crunch decision comes, if you don't trust the broker you won't take his or her advice, even if it's correct or appropriate. If you won't act on good counsel, then counsel is useless to you.

2. **A great broker knows and tells the truth**

   Truth is your friend; you may not like the truth, but you need to know it. A great broker will tell you the truth promptly, so you can act on it. A fabulous broker will tell you truth you need to know but you may not like. A shallow agent will only tell you what you want to hear; that lack of candor can waste your time, leave you a mediocre property, or produce a failed transaction. Here's one example of what telling the truth might sound like:

   Mr. Client, we both wish your building was worth two million dollars. Let's review the facts together. In fact, the bank appraiser will value it closer to $1,800,000....

A great broker tells the truth because he or she knows that truth is one of the pillars of trust. A single lie or omission of an important fact can bring that pillar crashing down and ruin a relationship.

You can't know enough about the work of your physician, attorney, or broker to evaluate the details of their work. Trust is your only option. In commercial real estate, we have codes of ethics to guide conduct, but an excellent broker should exceed the code. You want to build a relationship that will benefit both of you. That starts with telling the truth, and it grows if your broker always puts your interests first.

3. **A great broker, like a master teacher, knows and explains the market and the process**

To make wise choices, you need market information and a solid process for identifying, evaluating, buying, operating, and selling properties. Superior brokers will explain how things work so that you have the needed information. Mediocre brokers try to sell rather than partner with or develop a client. They see their role as presenting you with choices that you either accept or reject. A fabulous broker understands the responsibility to help you make a wise choice.

Excellent brokerage helps you understand and gain insights about the people and forces that you rarely deal with: principals on the other side of the table, competitors who want the same limited resources that you want, appraisers, brokers, lenders, and underwriters. Each of those groups is an integral part of the market. Your broker has to understand and communicate with each of them.

A skilled broker will explain why the transaction process works as it does. Even though apartment investors are wealthy, in this arena they are not special. Wealthy investors are competing with each other for properties and for buyers. Most sellers don't know even 10% of the brokers or 5% of the buyers. A well represented buyer may know 75% of the available properties, but probably does not know even 5% of his competitors.

In every field there are a few recognized elite players, far more people who are marginally competent, and some who are either incompetents or liars. The champions know and respect each other. They know who is trustworthy and, more important, who is not.

Some wise brokers can recognize and coach you though arbitrage opportunities. "Sell that building soon; the market is temporarily paying a huge premium for that area. Let's buy a property a couple of zip codes away. Briefly there is a glut. Jenkins is selling $10 million of property to meet his pledge to his college. They are naming a building after him." Smart brokers often recognize trends months or years ahead of their competitors and investors.

It takes immense wisdom and discipline to trust an expert. The most effective clients vet brokers diligently; and if the broker merits the trust, then they listen to counsel and act appropriately.

Your broker should know what you're looking for and translate that into zip codes and tangible characteristics so you recognize whether this particular building will do what you need.

Your star broker should help you understand why any asset will or won't accomplish your objective. Some properties look good and are in a nice neighborhood but may be poor choices for you. A superb broker's nuanced understanding provides the most appropriate asset for you and explains why that choice is superior.

For example, in San Diego County most apartment buildings don't have garages. So, obviously, units with garages earn higher rents. But there's another benefit that may not be so obvious. Tenants with nicer cars and who care about preserving property prefer a building with garages. So garages not only bring more income but also recruit better residents.

The new density bonus law created additional options if your property has garages. I thought I was paying attention when I read the density bonus law four times without understanding one of its major benefits. In some circumstances a rental owner can convert attached nonresidential space, like garages or carports into 25% of the number of permitted units and add two additional dwelling units. Some fourplexes with garages could by law convert garages to a fifth apartment and then build two more rentals. Maybe 10% of the rental parcels allow this jackpot conversion. Investors buy income property for income. Creating more rent checks creates more value.

A few smart, bold, and/or lucky investors will make phenomenal returns before this law sunsets. My guess is less than 10% of rental buyers between now and 2025 will benefit from this additional bonus detail.

This particular opportunity may not be available to you, but there will be great opportunities where you invest. Great brokers can enable an astute buyer to capture a superior opportunity.

4. **A great broker cushions clients from transaction speed bumps and shocks**

It would be nice if everything would go smoothly without surprises or problems, but that isn't the way life is. It's certainly not the way it is in investment real estate. A top broker warns you about future risks. A competent broker can insulate you from emotional stupidity, no matter where it originates. Setting realistic expectations reduces negative reactions. Here's an example of my "speed bump" talk to clients:

Ms. Client, sometime in this process, someone will insult you. Hopefully, it won't be our team. It may be the broker on the other side. It may be a lender, or the property manager or a tenant. But somebody may offend you. Then you'll have a perfectly good reason to say and to feel, "Don't you know who I am? I don't have to put up with this malarkey." And you can walk away mad and justified, or . . . you can be big enough and focused enough to ignore the incident and capture the superior property that will build wealth for decades. So, before you get insulted, consider what's best for your legacy.

A great broker will also be your shock absorber. I often get the emotion-filled call or email from the other side of a negotiation. Before I pass it on, I try to remove the flaming emotion and convey the business idea and some polite explanation of the other side's intensity.

5. **Superior brokers routinely accomplish remarkable results**
These paragraphs provide clues regarding what to look for when you choose a broker to partner with. You want a brokerage team that has proven how to close more or better or tougher transactions.

New flash—when millionaires compete for the limited number of superior options, your competition won't step aside so you can take your turn next. Average agents have pitiful results when competing against the champions. Some professionals get extra consideration, head starts, pricing guidance, private information from trade affiliates, second chances, and favors returned. It is not fair, but it is true. The best brokers work harder and smarter and spend a generation building relationships and helping others. They win a disproportionate percentage. Do you want the best working for you or against you?

Third-party awards can give you an idea of who the brokerage community thinks is excellent. San Diego County has 100+ agents who present themselves as apartment specialists. Rectums may win top producer at their firm, but they rarely win industry-wide awards. Industry recognition tends toward the nice professionals, not just the warriors with the most notches in their weapons. Our team has won more than a dozen county-wide awards for brokerage excellence, more than any other three teams. There is probably a broker with similar stand-out performance in your market.

High name recognition can indicate more successful brokers. Several radio programs have invited me to provide value to their affluent audience. The major owners in our market have received more than 100 mailers with my smiling face and have had access to 50 of my articles printed by a major business paper or apartment association journal. As a bonus, you can learn about a broker and his or her approach if you read their published articles.

Our team has some novel approaches that our worthy competition is not yet using. The best coaches have trick plays that are used only on high-stakes situations. You are best served by a team with some innovative techniques that give their client a competitive edge.

6. A great broker understands what you want and how you want to be remembered

There is a "what" and a "why" to building legacy wealth. The "what" is your investment goal and is related to your wealth. The "why" is about the way you want to be remembered. A terrific broker understands both and helps you achieve them. A champion broker "gets you" and your unique mix of goals and values.

You may have noticed that I haven't mentioned comparative fees. In most markets, the seller pays all the brokerage cost, even for the buy side. And, unlike the field of law, the best commercial real estate brokers don't charge five times as much as the run-of-the-mill. Amazingly, the best investment brokers charge about the same fee as the mediocre. The champions close deals that elude the mediocre.

How to Find the Broker Who's the Right Teammate for You

Here are some ways to find the best in your area. There is no perfect broker, no perfect spouse, no perfect child, and no perfect client. Be alert for the traits cited earlier. The more good traits you find in a broker, the better your chance of outrageous success. Research as if your future wealth depended on it.

Most of my excellent clients were referred by someone who knew both of us. Recommendations from people who know you and the broker well should be the gold standard. You will want to check them out further.

Your network may not link you directly to a premium broker. You have friends who invest, professional colleagues who could offer leads. Talk to income property appraisers, bankers, your CPA, rental owners, property managers, and your tax assessor. Ask the business or real estate editor of your local publication who the great brokers are. The local Realtor® group may have a commercial/investment division. Note the broker names you hear repeatedly. You may not know the best brain surgeon in your area code, but doctors and operating room nurses know the best one. Thoroughly investigate the agents who are mentioned repeatedly.

Your broker should have deep knowledge of apartment investing. Markets with populations above 2 million have more choices than cities below 500,000. In secondary markets, there may not be enough business to support all specialties. In smaller markets, income property agents might handle leasing and sale of office, retail, industrial, and multifamily. In markets with populations below 200,000 people, commercial brokerage is usually done by agents who mostly sell houses.

Check credentials and experience

Check credentials first. All commercial brokers are licensed, but fewer than 5% have earned the coveted Certified Commercial Investment Member (CCIM) designation. My MBA is helpful, but CCIM is specific for commercial real estate. After I was awarded my CCIM, I was able to prescribe solutions for situations I could not diagnose before.

CCIM is the premium designation for income property brokerage, the toughest of the Realtor® certifications. Your best choice may or may not be a CCIM.

Identify the finalists

Next, dig deeper into each broker's experience with a series of questions. Here are my suggestions; you will come up with others. Google them; ask the people in the field—appraisers, bankers, business or real estate section editors, trade associations, etc.—about them. You may not be able to answer all these questions for every broker, but you should learn enough to create a short list of finalists.

Do they specialize in investment real estate? How about in apartments?

Ask how many income properties they have closed. Brokers perfect their craft by closing deals. Every escrow in the last 25+ years has taught me how to serve clients better. The relative volume matters more than the actual number. Each market has unique transaction volume. Fifty escrows are a lot for Jacksonville, Florida, but not remarkable for San Diego. As of early 2018, our team has closed 400+ escrows and done 2,000+ property evaluations.

How many people are on their team? Seven people can do more work than two. Are they all white guys in ties speaking only English, or do they bring different cultural perspectives?

How many full economic cycles have they been through? I'm a better broker after having survived multiple recessions. In hard times, many agents wash out; flakes fail and never return. The wise and trustworthy remain. Experience teaches tough and important lessons about how to minimize risk and what not to do. Brokers are not proven until they have completed at least one full cycle.

How many long-term clients do they serve? Great brokers develop long-term relationships with their clients. The longer the relationship, the better the relationship, the more deals they do, and the smoother things can go. Stephen M. R. Covey's, *The Speed of Trust,* says this:

> Trust always affects two quantifiable variables: speed and cost. Trust equals confidence. When trust goes down in a relationship or a company, speed goes down and cost goes up. When trust goes up, speed goes up and cost goes down. Trust always impacts speed and cost.

To make his point, Covey tells the story of Warren Buffett and his purchase of McLane Distribution. In 2003, Buffett agreed to buy the company from Walmart after a single meeting. In his annual letter to shareholders, Buffett said that he did almost no due diligence before agreeing to the purchase because he trusted Walmart. Trust made it possible to close a deal quickly that would have taken battalions of attorneys months to accomplish.

Trust will have the same impact on your pursuit of legacy wealth. As you work with a great broker and build your relationship, trust will increase. That, in turn, makes it possible for you to move faster and seize opportunities you might miss otherwise.

How do they act when they make a mistake? Everybody goofs. You and your broker will both make mistakes. How mistakes are handled has a huge impact on the relationship. Top-performing brokers acknowledge mistakes and then promptly and energetically make things right. It may seem counterintuitive, but that strengthens the relationship.

When a broken bone mends, the spot of the break is stronger than the rest of the bone. The same thing is true of business relationships. According to the customer satisfaction research firm, TARP, "Customers who complain and are satisfied are up to 8% more loyal than if they had no problem at all." Marriott studied guests who reported a problem during their stay. If Marriott took action to make things right, 94% of those guests were even more likely to return to Marriott, as compared to the 89% return rate of guests who had no problem at all.

Your research can generate a short list of brokers to consider partnering with. The next step is to meet them. The in-person interview will help you make the best choice possible.

Prepare for the interview

Review your research notes and prepare a list of questions. The candidate's answers can help you make a smart choice.

You're deciding whether to work with the broker. Many brokers expect the interview to be a sales situation. Brokers approach these meetings in either of two ways.

Some brokers try to persuade you to hire them. They try to sell you. These brokers will usually ask fewer questions and listen less. Expect the same treatment if you become their client.

Client-centered brokers, on the other hand, want you to make a wise decision about whether you should work together. They are also making that decision themselves. They will usually ask more questions and listen to what you say. Expect them to engage more with you if you work with them.

Have specific questions for each broker. Ask each one: "If I choose you as our broker, how will we proceed?" Different brokers work in different ways. This book shows one terrific way to select the best option. Other professionals may prefer a different system. Please let me know about systems that may seem better to you or to your broker.

One last truth: The best broker might not take you as a client. Years ago, I invested in another state. The top broker politely explained my budget was too small for him to work on. Obtain the best broker you can find.

There are many benefits to teaming with your broker. Your team may include your spouse or significant other, a business partner, a property manager, and your broker. Usually two (or three or four) heads are better than one. Teamwork's best benefit is that teaming increases the likelihood of achieving your goals.

Not all teams are productive, though, so let's review what research tells us about top-performing teams of all kinds.

What a Terrific Team Looks Like

More and more of the world's work is done by teams. Researchers have sought to discover what separates the magnificent from the mediocre.

In the last few years, researchers from MIT and from Google have developed good descriptions of business teams where both productivity and morale are high. Here's my synthesis of their findings, adapted for broker-client teams.

Great teams have clear goals. You bring draft goals. A great broker can help you sharpen your goals. The team's goals should be to help you build legacy wealth and help you define what that means.

Great teams have strong processes. The broker should have a rigorous, systematic process for analyzing opportunities and for buying and selling property. Later in the book, you will learn my process to help clients evaluate opportunities and structure deals.

Great teams have full participation. Your meetings should be conversations, with both you and your broker sharing information and insights and listening to each other. Researchers at Google coined the term "psychological safety" to describe the way the highly productive teams work. Another way to say that is that members of top teams are emotionally mature.

Great teams build trust. Trust doesn't happen automatically or overnight. Instead, trust grows interaction by interaction. You should trust your broker to show you every listing that meets your criteria and give you his or her best professional judgment about properties and strategies. Your broker should trust you to share relevant things that matter to you. Both of you build trust by telling and hearing the truth.

How to Be a Great Client and Teammate

Superior brokers have more demand than they can fulfill. How do you become a client that your broker loves doing business with? What would make you a great teammate for your broker?

Know what you want. You're the only one who knows your values and what matters to you. And you're the only one who can decide whether a particular opportunity is right for you. A great broker can help deepen

your understanding and help you understand the consequences of different decisions, but you're the only one who can make the decision that's
right for you.

Your goals are likely to change over time as your life changes and
as you become a more experienced and sophisticated investor. Even so,
things will go better if you know what's important to you and you have
clear goals.

Show you're part of a team. Participate in the process. Do your
homework. Provide clear and candid feedback. Ask about other options
that you find. The best brokers probably already know about most of what
you discover, but they will welcome your questions as part of the process
of educating you. Keep your promises. Bring your broker in on potential
opportunities you find on your own.

Pull the trigger. You won't build legacy wealth by sitting on the
sidelines. Great clients make offers and close.

Teaming up with a fabulous broker is the key to building legacy wealth
over the long term. Since you will be investing again and again, you will
get better results if you have a process or system you can use every time.
You'll learn about that in the next chapter.

Make Sure You Have a System That Will Work for You Every Time

"The secret of success in life, is for men to be ready for his opportunity when it comes."
~ Benjamin Disraeli

IN THE BEGINNING, the Roman Army was like all the other contemporary armies, but it became world-conquering because of the systems they developed for every aspect of military life and waging battle.

Other armies stopped for the night and their commanders figured out how to set up camp. The Romans had a process for that, so they set up camp the same way every time. Roman camps always had effective fortifications, a secure water supply, and sentries assigned to guard duty. Roman soldiers were drilled in how to respond to a surprise attack, so everyone knew what to do.

Roman soldiers weren't any braver or stronger than other soldiers. Their leaders weren't smarter than the leaders of other armies. Developing "best practices" made it possible for Roman soldiers to do great things. Those "recipes for action" that the army used repeatedly made it possible for the Romans to implement whatever strategies they chose. Tech geeks speak about algorithms; real estate investors call them processes or systems.

A process or investing system is a series of steps designed to achieve a specific outcome. Effective, repeatable processes, combined with knowing what you want and understanding the market, are the core of an effective strategy. I've developed processes for every phase of the wealth escalator, though I customize the details for every client.

You don't need to conquer the world, but repeatable processes will help you achieve your legacy wealth goals. Having an effective process is critical if you intend to build your legacy wealth. In this chapter, you'll learn how strong processes make it possible to develop winning strategies, just like they did for the Roman Army. I'll also introduce you to the two things you must know to create an effective wealth-building strategy and keep it fresh.

A process facilitates communication and accountability. My clients and I know our roles and what to expect of each other. I'm responsible for the technical research that identifies properties that meet their basic requirements. My clients are responsible for reviewing the properties. Together, we decide which properties to pursue and the offer price for each.

A process functions like a checklist. We always complete all the steps to obtain the best results.

A process focuses your attention on the most important things. Psychologists have a concept called "cognitive load" that refers to the amount of thinking your brain does. Using the same process means we're not reinventing the wheel, but simply working with known tools. We focus our mental resources on selecting the wealth building properties.

The process really does make it better. For most people, making any large purchase is not playing on a level field. Think about buying a car. The car dealer knows more about cars than you do, especially the car they're trying to sell to you. And, very likely, they have much more experience and skill at negotiating. My process gives our clients a huge edge over clients with only mediocre representation.

Legacy wealth doesn't usually accrue in one investment. It takes several escrows over many years. Effective processes help you and your broker *routinely* make smart decisions based on what's possible. The more you work together, the more you learn about each other, and the better your decisions should become. That understanding gives you an immense edge over less informed, but maybe more affluent buyers.

First-time buyers usually think about only one deal. The first purchase is smaller than what they'll do later, and it doesn't automatically dawn on them that this is something they're going to repeat for decades. Done well, income property investing will do more for their financial future than their day job.

Since you're reading this book, you think about the long-term. That's good. That will help you choose a broker who has a strong process that can improve with every transaction. Clarifying your values and goals, deepening your market understanding, and embracing investing realities will boost your investment success, effectively and with lower risk.

Know What You Really Want

Over the years, unhappy investors have told me about bad experiences with other brokers. Again and again, I've heard some variant of "That broker *sold* me a property and . . ." followed by something awful. If you've followed my advice and chosen a great broker, that's far less likely to happen because a top broker understands that his or her job is to help you make wise decisions, not to sell you a property. Even with a first-rate broker and good advice, you could still make awful decisions if you aren't clear about your objectives and what's important to you.

There are no investments that are great for everyone. Apartments might be perfect for one investor but might be inappropriate for another investor with different objectives.

Consider one of my favorite investors, a 35-year-old firefighter. His apartments are the "family farm"; he does a lot of the work. He became a millionaire in five years of working with our team. His right investment might be an ugly building in a scary zip code because he can grow wealth quickly by fixing common problems himself.

But what if you're that same firefighter's 79-year-old uncle? You've made your fortune. Once you worked like your nephew, but now you want something that won't demand much time and attention. So, your best option might be a beach property with modest cash flow, but one that requires almost no attention. Your best investment might not even be another apartment building, but instead a building leased by a national drug store chain, where all you must do is cash the rent checks.

I'm amazed that so many wealth-building writers skimp on clarity of goals. A pilot who arrived quickly at the wrong airport would be in trouble and so would his passengers. Get clear about your objectives and what's important to you. That clarity will dramatically increase the possibility that you will build legacy wealth. Remember the wisdom given by Socrates or Plato: "Know thyself."

That was hard for the ancient Greeks, and it may be hard for you. Knowing yourself doesn't come naturally. You must clarify your values, your legacy ambition, your investment goals, and how you will make the trade-offs you will confront. That isn't always easy, but it can be doubly hard if you discover that you and your spouse differ on key issues. Then the two of you will have to negotiate those differences.

Recently I met with a couple where he was leaning one way and she was inclined another. Once I understood their concerns and objectives, my challenge was to clearly and tangibly explain the various trade-offs. Over time, they will decide which options to pursue.

Recognize that your thinking and goals may change as you age and as your skills and expertise shift. More information often changes expectations and choices between the trade-offs.

An important part of selecting a goal is deciding what secondary or tertiary benefit you'll give up, or what you'll pay to attain the primary advantage.

Learn about the Market and Submarkets

If you don't understand the market, you can't make wise investment decisions no matter how clear you are about your values and investment goals. Not only that, without your own market knowledge, you're at the mercy of your broker and you're not in control of your own wealth building. Knowing the market means more than simply reading about it.

First-time buyers, novices, have a different challenge than repeat investors, apprentices, journeymen, or master craftsmen. New buyers need to spend "windshield time," driving different neighborhoods. An afternoon may help you understand why one zip code sells for 10% more than the neighboring zip code. The properties, cars, clothing, and recreation tell you a lot about the neighborhood, the income, and education level of the residents.

Before you start making investment decisions, you should spend windshield time driving the markets to see the realities. Google Earth is fine for some things, but first you need to be there in person. Spend 40 hours driving potential investment neighborhoods, and that time will pay off far more than an extra week's income. When you learn the market that way, you'll increase your chance of wise choices. Reality is routinely different from the cropped photos that appear in the marketing brochures. Expert investors, like expert brokers, have learned through a couple of economic cycles. Hint: that means inviting your heirs to pay attention to you, your investments, and your decision making . . . before your will is read.

Your goal is to learn what the people and properties are like in different areas so you can recognize a bargain and understand the implications of owning in various neighborhoods.

Start with a list from your broker of properties that have recently sold or are for sale now. Your goal is to learn the differences among various neighborhoods. Driving possible investment zip codes looking at recent sales and properties for sale provides the discernment which enables wiser investment choices.

Begin by going out in the middle of the day during the work week. What are the buildings like? How well are they maintained? Is there new construction, or somebody cleaning up, painting up, fixing up, doing additions, or remodeling? New money coming into the neighborhood is a good thing.

Look at the parking lots. Empty parking lots may mean tenants are at work. Full parking lots may imply government subsidized non-working tenants. Or maybe several tenants work the night shift. Look at the cars. Are they nice or junky? Is anyone doing auto maintenance on the street?

Take notes so you don't have to rely on your fallible human memory. Invite your spouse or significant other; two heads are better than one. Compare your reactions and discuss the neighborhoods. When you get home, research the neighborhoods you visited. Compare crime statistics from local law enforcement websites. Pay special attention to domestic violence, robberies, and murders.

Go back to the neighborhoods at night. Are people out in the streets or in their homes? What does it sound like? Visit the same neighborhood on Sunday morning. The residue of Saturday night activities may be visible Sunday morning.

Stretch your understanding of the market as much as possible. Look at a wider range of zip codes than you think is necessary. Several of my most successful clients did superbly in areas that were not on their first list of target zip codes. Spending a few hours investigating some extra areas will increase your chance of making terrific choices. Look in more areas and at more properties than you can buy.

When you understand the differences between submarkets, you'll make better investment decisions. Over time you'll develop your own gut instinct about properties, and that will make you a better investor and a better client.

Your excellent broker should provide basic processes to identify, evaluate, and seize opportunities and to modify those processes to fit your needs and goals. He or she will understand the market and the players. But to get the most from your broker, you should learn about some apartment-investing realities that may not be immediately obvious. That's what you'll do in the next chapter.

Apartment Investing Realities

"There are no solutions. There are only trade-offs."
~ THOMAS SOWELL

"Risk is equally common to action and inaction."
~ GENERAL AL GRAY

INVESTING IN APARTMENTS IS A SPLENDID WAY to build legacy wealth. But before we move on to specific investing techniques, let's consider some realities. Too many investors never achieved the results that were possible for them. They were smart; they had the resources; they said they wanted to invest in apartments. But that wasn't enough.

Often, they didn't succeed because they didn't understand some important realities. This chapter is based on actual investor conversations regarding these realities.

The truth is that you can understand everything else in this book, have all the resources you need, and still fail if you don't understand these things. Just suppose you were gaining wise counsel from a proven guide, a fellow with a huge smile and some deep scars testifying to expensive lessons. Remember this:

It is your money.

Too many investors have complained that some broker "sold me" a property that wasn't a good choice. If you don't know the market, you might decide based on someone else's opinion about what's a good investment for you. On the positive side, developing your own market sense and what properties are right for you will make you a better teammate for your broker.

It's *your* money, not the broker's cash, not your friend's capital. *You* choose. Seek wise counsel, but recognize that it is your choice. A great broker will seek to understand you and your goals and the properties that will work for you. Then he or she will tell you about those properties and not distract you with inappropriate options. The longer you work together, the better you and your broker will become at identifying properties that fit your goals. That's a learning process for your broker and for you.

Apartment Investing Is a Learning Journey

When you were a newly minted high school graduate, you didn't know what all the work possibilities and realities were. During college, you may have changed your major more than once as you learned more about yourself and the possibilities. When you got into the work world, you probably changed jobs at least once, and maybe you even changed careers. Expect a similar learning process as you build legacy wealth.

Many first-time investors start with market fantasies and inaccurate expectations about being a landlord. That's normal. Most investors change their ideas as they learn about the market and the realities of the market and landlording.

You learn by doing, whether you're riding a bike, swimming, mastering your job, or landlording. This learning step is necessary, but without smart preparation it can involve unnecessarily costly lessons. It's prudent to do your homework, such as reading this book. Low risk means avoiding folly, unnecessary risk. Then, the best way to learn about market reality is the windshield time I described in the last chapter.

Every apartment building is unique. You can't understand the differences unless you analyze many opportunities. Landlording is a contact sport. You can't learn what it's like just by reading or by analyzing a spreadsheet. You must get out and go and see. You learn by doing deals and confronting unfamiliar situations.

Cost and Value

Years ago, one of my friends had a side business buying oak furniture in New England and selling it on the West Coast. At the time, people in New England associated oak furniture with brothels and cheap hotels. They were glad to have my friend take it off their hands and pay them actual money for it.

My friend transported the furniture to the West Coast. He cleaned it up and polished it. Then he sold it to people who paid relatively high prices for it because it was trendy at the time. The key word in that last sentence is "relatively."

Profit is the difference between cost and sales price. Relative value compares the potential profit for different investments. Suppose you visited a mine and had just enough cash to buy an ounce of gold for 95% of the current price. Now suppose that you discovered you could buy a pound of silver for the same price. The cost is the same; which is the best value?

Checking the current sale price would reveal which element—gold or silver—would bring the most cash. Apartment investing works the same way: You want to invest in the opportunity that will give you the greatest profit when you sell. The question is not which zip code has the highest income residents or highest education. Instead the question is which zip code will be the most profitable for you.

You build your legacy wealth faster when you invest in properties with the biggest difference between your cost and what the next buyer will pay. Because our team is hyperactive, we know a zip code where a buyer must spend $30K per unit to raise rents 30% and another zip code just 5 miles away where only $15K upgrades can bring an income of 30% more. More bang for the buck is the better value. Buildings that have the right things wrong with them (fixable problems) enable you to create value. The wise investor finds the opportunity with bigger profit potential. When it comes time to sell your property, you and your broker will pick the list price based on what a reasonable buyer would pay for it.

Improving property should improve net income and thus boost value. The best returns are those that generate relatively higher return on the investment.

The Best Investments Probably Won't Be Where You Live

Each month, an investor says something like this:

> I want to make the most money possible, so I want to invest in the best areas. The residents in those areas earn more, so they can pay higher rents and the vacancy rate will be less.

It's true that renters in the "best areas" earn more and can pay higher rents. And it's true that the vacancy rate in the "best areas" will probably be lower. But that isn't the whole story; and because it isn't, the conclusion is wrong. Smart apartment investors who want to build wealth don't always buy property in the top third of zip codes. More than half of those wealth-building investors buy in the zip codes in the bottom third of the socioeconomic continuum.

There are three kinds of areas in any market. The top third are the upscale areas; in San Diego, these are areas that are close to salt water or office buildings. The bottom third consists of the "challenged" zip codes.

They're the ones more likely to get mentioned on the nightly news. They're also the zip codes where you'll find the most opportunity to build your legacy wealth.

You may be thinking that the upscale property will generate more cash flow. Rents are higher, but investors pay a high premium to own property in a top zip code.

Bear with me a bit. There isn't much math in this book, and this example is about as complicated as it gets. In San Diego, investors who buy beach assets pay two or three times as much per apartment, or 40% more per rent dollar for that pride of ownership. Suppose an ordinary zip code sells for $200K a unit, say, 14 times the income. The beach rents for more. Beach property might sell for 19 times the (higher) annual rents, or $400K per apartment.

Your cash can buy a medium-sized property in an ordinary zip code or a small asset in a fancy zip code. If both increase at about the same rate, then the larger asset, the one in the ordinary zip code, will increase by a greater dollar amount. Here's an example.

Suppose you have $750K for a down payment. You could buy a $1.5 million property in a beach zip code or a $2.25 million building in an ordinary zip code. Let's say that both appreciate 20%. Your beach $1.5 million grows $300K, which is wonderful! Alternatively, your ordinary $2.25 million increases $450K. Wealth builders know that an increase of $450K in your property is better than $300K.

To understand why investment opportunities are more common in the lowest third of zip codes, you don't need math—just common sense. If you were paying a premium rent for a place in a fancy zip code, what would you expect? You'd expect the building to be in excellent condition, the fixtures and finishes to be top notch. If you were the owner of a building like that, what could you do to improve the value? The answer is, not much.

In the lowest third zip codes, that isn't the case. That larger upside offers greater potential opportunity to create legacy wealth. Leverage and improvability make zip codes in the bottom third the place where savvy investors go to build wealth.

The wealthy mentor summarized for his protégé: Invest where you won't live, and live where you won't invest.

Renters and Owners Are in Different Economic Positions

If you want to make the most money, expect to rent to people who are different from you. They almost certainly will have less money. Low-income people are more likely to be renters. They don't have big saving accounts or debt-free new cars. Rental owners are not better people, but we do have more and better economic choices.

My clients have shown me that their profit is maximized by renting to people who are different from owners. Your residents may make different choices about how they cook, how they save, how they spend, how they vote, or how they worship. Those differences make some people uncomfortable, but they're part of the realities of apartment investing.

Apartment Investing Is Like NASCAR Driving, Not Having a Nordstrom Shopper

Let's face it, if you can afford to buy apartment buildings, you are wealthy. People who know your financial capacity treat you well in most sales situations. If you're going spend a lot at Nordstrom, they can provide a personal shopper, who screens clothes based on your best colors and specific shape. Give a sales clerk a load of money for a decreasing-value asset such as clothing or a new car, and they will suck up to you. Investing in apartments is different; it's more like the hurly-burly competition of NASCAR driving.

When you invest in apartments, you will deal with another affluent person, someone who will probably never deal with you again. He or she does not care whether you like the purchase experience or whether you tell your friends about your impressions. The seller may not dispose of another building for 10 years. Your social media posting does not matter to his income-property success. The seller may deal with scores of tenants each month and a buyer once a decade. Your opinion won't be noticed by or be relevant to the seller's tenants. Other potential investors are unlikely to ever encounter the seller you're dealing with.

If you want a great deal, you can't afford to be fragile, or easily bruised. You are buying an income stream. NASCAR drivers aren't genteel and polite on the track; they cut things close, and they may push another driver into the wall. Spending money on luxury is a different mindset from outmaneuvering other smart, motivated investors to obtain a superior income stream for life.

If you want to be pampered, get a massage. A better investment choice can pay for years of massages.

There Are Always Trade-Offs

Which do you prefer, steak or pizza? Your answer depends on your goal. If you're having friends over on Sunday afternoon to watch football, pizza might be the choice. You probably wouldn't choose it for an important anniversary dinner, though. Trade-offs mean choices. If your goal is to build legacy wealth, your choice will be different than if your goal is to maximize cash flow or own a property with little management hassle and predictable cash flow for the next 20 years.

Trade-offs mean picking your hard. To build legacy wealth you will invest money, thought, and time now to reap wealth and better choices later. Every purchase decision will have trade-offs. As I said earlier, it would be nice if there was a "sit on the couch, eat ice cream, gain muscle, and lose weight" diet, but there isn't. It would be nice if you could find the "perfect" property, too, but you won't. Some properties are better for your goals, while others don't take you where you want to go.

I'm a triathlete, but I'm unwilling to spend 20 hours and $200 a week for coaching to do 12 intense workouts each week. The guys on the podium earn that glory because they pay more for their triathlons. They are happy about that, and I'm happy for them. They picked that hard; they have not written a book. Each person picks his or her own hard.

Trade-offs are about deciding what you will put up with to get something else you want. Perhaps you will invest in buildings in "less desirable" neighborhoods because they offer you more upside than other properties. What problems can and will you fix? What risks will you accept?

There may be trade-offs at home, too. No matter how compatible you and your spouse are, you will have differences. Sometimes that trade-off is between two properties that each of you thinks is a great choice. Mark and Sharon deal with that by having Mark visit the properties and Sharon having veto power. Deciding comes from a root word which means *to cut off*. Deciding means you decline most options to capture another option.

Sometimes the trade-off is deciding whether to act or not. There are only a limited number of apartment properties on the market at any time. You don't get to pick from all the apartments in your area—just the ones for sale. You may decide that nothing on the market right now meets your goals. That's OK sometimes, but if you never buy, you're not an investor; you're a spectator. Spectators pay to watch, but never receive any prize.

The One Important Thing That Brings It All Together

"A bias for action." Tom Peters and Bob Waterman coined that phrase in their book, *In Search of Excellence,* to describe the successful companies they profiled. My experience is that it's characteristic of successful apartment investors, too.

Superior investors review their investments regularly and decide when it's time to exchange up. I send them a list of properties that I think will work, and they review the list and rank the properties. Many investors complete all of that in a week. We write multiple offers. You'll learn more about how and why that works in the chapter, Successful Buying.

Great clients have the end in mind and decide quickly. They know what they want and that we'll have enough due diligence time to evaluate the opportunity. They make offers, inspect, negotiate, and decide whether to buy or not. They close.

I've worked with people who combed through lists of opportunities looking for the perfect building. Of course, they never found it because there is no such thing. Others have expressed curiosity and wanted full due diligence before making any offers. They never put any property into escrow. Both sets of people are spectators, not competitors. Perhaps they find it entertaining, or maybe they are still toying with the idea.

Nimble and motivated buyers close. They make the best choices they can in an imperfect world and they get on with it. Let me put it differently. When Steve Jobs was the CEO of Apple, many people described him as an artist and a perfectionist. He probably was, given all the great products he brought to the world, but he constantly reminded the people at Apple that designing great products was not enough. Neither was waiting to act until the product was perfect. One of his mantras was "Great artists ship!"

Great investors close.

More than 2,000 millionaires who did not yet own apartments have told me they wanted and expected to buy San Diego apartments. After reviewing the ownership records, it appears that only about 10% of them actually bought apartments. If you desire to be among the minority who build legacy wealth, you must close escrows. The next section will describe tools you will use to invest profitably in apartments.

The Wealth Escalator

The next six chapters explain what you will do routinely as you build your legacy wealth. They outline the process of buying a property with the right things wrong with it, improving it, and selling it.

First, **A Practical Way to Prioritize Opportunities** shows you how to identify the best investment options among a host of properties.

Successful Buying describes my method for making offers on several properties, rather than just one, and why writing back-up offers can help you capture an opportunity you thought was gone.

Successful Operating is an introduction to landlording. You'll discover the important choices you will make and how rental ownership can affect your legacy.

Renovation Budgets and Strategies teaches about a vital "Power Tool of Investing." You'll learn how and when to develop renovation budgets that increase the value of your property and help you build legacy wealth.

Successful Selling explains how to decide when it's time to sell and the aspects of human nature that may lead to poor selling decisions. You'll also learn how to price and market your property, and how to develop offers into successful closings.

The next chapter describes an indispensable wealth building tool, **1031 Exchange.** This portion of IRS code enables rental owners to defer taxes and keep all your capital working for you and growing.

This section's final chapter, **Wealth Escalator Summary**, concludes what's been discussed in this section.

A Practical Way to Prioritize Opportunities

"He who chases two rabbits catches none."
~ Anonymous

"The drudgery of numbers will make you free."
~ Harold Geneen

Investing intelligently in apartments is hard work if you do it right, yet it can produce legacy wealth. Casual investing can be financially dangerous. Spending money is easy and fun, but it doesn't help you build legacy wealth. Investing wisely can be extremely rewarding. Extremely rewarding! Wise apartment investing begins with assessing what properties you can afford.

Start with how much cash you have available for a down payment, closing costs, and upgrades, if we find the best opportunity on today's market. For the sake of discussion, assume you could find $500K if you could capture the best deal. That does not mean $500K for the down payment alone. You might use $405K for the down payment and $5K for closing costs, with an available $90K for additional improvements to the property in the first year.

Candidly, the $90K for upgrades does not have to be in the bank now, but you need to expect that it will come from income or from the sale of other assets within the next year. I may ask you if you could find another $30K as a cushion, just in case there was a surprise.

Wait! That feels like mission creep. The buyer said $500K and the broker is trying to get $530K! Well, welcome to the world of improving property. Often things take longer and cost more than you expect.

Maybe you ultimately decide that $500K is your maximum, and we look for an asset that you can buy with $395K down plus closing costs. You'll budget $85K for upgrades and commit to use some income from other sources so that you will have $20K as a liquidity cushion.

Investing wisely in apartments involves discovering almost all the current plausible options, prioritizing them, writing several offers, negotiating counteroffers, and hopefully being able to inspect two, or maybe three, of the best candidates. There will often be a final haggle after the property inspection. You obtain the financing and then close on your best option. Each step, done well, requires intelligence and focus.

If your market only has three options, then you can skip this chapter. Maybe you're looking in the wrong market or maybe your focus is too tight. In San Diego County, there are usually 100–400 apartment buildings for sale worth $750K or more.

In this chapter, you'll learn how my process blends systematic, low-tech analysis with your personal emotional and economic goals and available options. You'll discover some tips about effective decision making, and you'll be introduced to the prioritizing tool I developed to help my clients recognize superior wealth-building opportunities.

Fair warning: There is work involved, for you and your broker. Think of it as a temporary part-time job. This part-time job can pay you three to five times your regular hourly rate, and there is no income tax due on the rewards.

There is more than one way to win. Few people have the gift of vision; these people can see past an ugly reality and draw on an almost magical ability to creatively adapt a structure. Well-trained or gifted architects and artistic personalities sometimes see possibilities that ordinary mortals can't grasp. If you are that blessed, great for you!

For the 90% of us without that special gift, these pages provide a low-tech way to identify potential value among a host of ordinary looking properties.

The Assessment Process

This process can start in different ways. Some clients review their holdings regularly, decide when it's time to trade up, and contact me. Sometimes I contact them first, either because I've identified an opportunity that I think will interest them or because it seems like time to trade up. Sometimes another broker might present an opportunity to them and they bring it to me.

No matter how it starts, the assessment process is essentially the same, regardless of the number of properties. I'd like all my clients to do what I'm describing in this chapter, but some don't. Purposeful and systematic investors use this process and obtain far better results.

This prioritizing system focuses clients on the opportunities that are most likely to build wealth. The goal is to buy the best available option during our search period. That goal is different from finding the cheapest price or the best location or prettiest asset or the best alternative this decade.

To find our client's best choice, I need to understand our client, but I don't have to agree with him or her. Often smart people don't know what they don't know about buying apartments. Our team identifies assets that will accomplish their goals. Often clients discover and articulate preferences or concerns that they had not previously articulated or recognized.

While I was writing this book, a smart couple rejected four properties that did not fit them. Each property was a good opportunity, but the couple was more risk averse than most of my clients; they needed an opportunity where they had high control over the structural risk. There was a learning process for those buyers and for me.

Three of the assets they declined to buy were on private roads. One asset had some unusual settlement issues. Clay soil had gotten wet, causing settlement. The seller had corrected most of the drainage issues, the ground would gradually dry out and the structure would settle back in the drier soil. Different clients, who had no qualms about the private road or unusual settlement issues, bought three of the four rejected properties. The buyers of those three are quite happy with their purchases.

The point of that story is to learn what matters to you. Both the clients who rejected the buildings and those who bought made the correct choices for them. Nordstrom sells suits in more than one size; what's great for a tall person is wrong for a short person.

The goal is also to identify the best value, from what's available now. Sometimes a perfectly good building is sold because the seller needs the cash. Perhaps the seller's motivation may come from retirement, health issues, divorce, or trading up. The best opportunity is different from the best property or the best neighborhood. We choose the best investment possibility for our client after analyzing the available opportunities.

Remember, the ideal investment is a property with the right things wrong with it. The right things are solvable problems—things where the fix adds value. In contrast, some problems cost money but don't add value. Replacing the roof or sewer system costs a lot, but it doesn't bring more rent.

Some problems can't be fixed economically. When there's a railroad track right behind the property and freight trains roar through around 2:00 AM, even triple-pane windows can't stop the noise. Likewise, you also can't fix an underparked building.

Parking needs vary from city to city and neighborhood to neighborhood. Every city has people without cars who get around with taxis, ride-share services, and public transportation. But where people need a car, the car needs a parking place. Tenants with two cars don't like apartments with only one parking space per apartment. The owner usually can't add parking.

Most structural problems, like a broken foundation where structural integrity is compromised, are the wrong kind of problems for most investors. If you're the right kind of engineer or contractor, you might be able to make money by solving problems that most others could not solve economically. In our county, minor cracks in foundations are routine nuisances of little economic significance.

We want a building where your capital expenditure enables you to boost rents. Changing the paint color from ugly to stylish can bring higher rents. Updating faucets, fixtures, drawer pulls, knobs, and ceiling fans to currently fashionable is a good investment. Refacing the cabinet doors, installing new countertops, and upgrading flooring usually create value.

Sometimes, changing management can add value. The previous management may have done poor credit checking or may not have enforced house rules. If sellers skipped maintenance, like fixing leaky toilets or were rude to the tenants, those blunders may create wealth opportunities when you use simple good-management practices.

In summary, we're looking for the best opportunity from the available options to build legacy wealth. Let's consider a tool that focuses attention on a manageable number of options.

The Source of Possible Opportunities

I create the list of possible opportunities for my clients. Your broker should do it for you, but don't be surprised if he or she has never displayed your options in a spreadsheet before.

This unique spreadsheet simplifies your decision making by ranking your options. The process prioritizes potential opportunities for our clients. We gather information from the multiple listing service and Internet sites, and we add other properties that are not fully marketed but might be bought for a sensible price. That starting point may have 7 or 27 options, depending the client's capital, target area, and other factors.

Next, we exclude the overpriced properties and others that seem to have less than a 50/50 chance of selling in the next 6 months. Often that eliminates a third of the buildings.

Some clients make an extra step. Recall the process Mark and Sharon and I use and which I described in the chapter, Team Up with a Great Broker. First, we generate a preliminary list of possibilities; then Mark drives the market and looks at each property. He and Sharon whittle down the list some more.

The key financial and physical details of the remaining buildings are summarized on a spreadsheet. Then we highlight the top third of the properties on each key metric. Here's a look at the tool in detail.

The Assessment Tool

Here's an example of our Assessment Tool.

This assessment tool enables clients to extract the best potential options from a blizzard of numbers. It prioritizes and helps investors quickly recall key details. Here's what all the columns are about.

The first column is the **Property Address, City, and Zip Code**.

Column two shows the **List Price**. It's the seller's asking price, or it may be the last known counteroffer price.

Number of Units is next. There's also a breakdown of the Unit Mix on the far right of the sheet. I'll describe that in a moment.

$/Unit is simple math; List Price divided by the Number of Units.

$/SqFt is calculated by dividing the List Price by the "rentable square footage" from the county tax assessor's records.

GRM is Gross Rent Multiple. It's the listing price divided by the Gross Scheduled Income (GSI), which is how much you could collect if there was full occupancy and no vacancy or bad check loss. A building that potentially generates $100K of gross revenue and sells for $1.2 million has a GRM of 12 times the annual rent. If that property with its $100K of potential income

COMPETING PROPERTIES FOR BOB BUYER

#	Property Address City, Zip	List Price Comments	# of Units	At List Price $/Unit	$/SqFt	GRM*	Cap Rate	Year Built	Number of Garages	Stu	1Br	2Br	3-Br	Suggested Offer
1	**9737 Apple Ave Lakeside, 92040**	$3,300,000 New cabinets, countertops in kitchen and baths	11	$300,000	**$289**	**11.0**	**6.6%**	**1991**	**5**	0	0	0	**11**	**$3,200,000**
2	2870 Orange San Diego, 92102	$2,400,000 Walking distance from downtown	9	**$266,667**	$392	19.4	2.7%	1964	0	0	9	0	0	
3	3041 Pear St San Diego, 92102	$2,750,000 Close to Balboa Park, Zoo, and downtown	10	**$275,000**	$404	16.5	3.6%	1987	**3**	0	7	1	2	
4	4157 Lemon St San Diego, 92104	$3,350,000 Close to freeways and local restaurants	8	$418,750	$606	16.1	4.1%	1987	0	0	3	**5**	0	
5	**4070 Grape St San Diego, 92105**	$1,750,000 6 garages for extra income	6	$291,667	**$322**	**12.8**	**5.3%**	**1988**	**6**	0	0	**2**	**4**	**$1,650,000**
6	**4380 Banana Ave San Diego, 92105**	$3,190,000 3 Garages and onsite laundry facilities with owned equipment	11	$290,000	**$391**	15.4	4.0%	1972	**3**	0	4	**7**	0	**$2,870,000**
7	**4157 Berry St San Diego, 92105**	$1,575,000 7 condos with garages	7	**$225,000**	$402	**13.7**	**4.5%**	**2007**	**7**	0	6	0	1	**$1,499,000**
8	4638-4648 Mango Ave San Diego, 92116	$5,600,000 Massive upgrades—can be operated as two 8 units	16	$350,000	$529	16.4	3.8%	1982	**4**	0	6	**10**	0	
9	4515 Papaya Ln San Diego, 92116	$2,430,000 A block from Adams Ave	8	$303,750	$507	15.5	4.0%	1968	0	0	5	3	0	

sells for $1.5 million, it has a GRM of 15. This simple sorting measure is good enough to develop a list of semifinalists. Nationally, CCIMs use the synonym term Gross Potential Income. For my San Diego readers, I'm citing the Southern California term, GRM, that my market uses.

Cap Rate, or Capitalization Rate, is the buyer's net operating income divided by the List Price. Net operating income is the cash flow after all the cash expenses have been deducted from the cash income. Net operating income, or NOI, ignores appreciation or depreciation or mortgage payment. Cap rate can be a more precise measure than GRM, but it isn't always helpful. Most apartment properties have unaudited financials. Remember GIGO—garbage in, garbage out. Recognize that some brokers are great; others are marginally competent. Some owners are honest with the tax man; others forget to report laundry income and some rents. Some landlords shop insurance annually and buy appliances with damage that can't be seen; others are sloppy with the expenses. In other words, don't fixate on trivia at this early stage. The mismanaged property may have the best profit potential.

Cap Rate might be meaningless because the owner's brother-in-law does the plumbing and is paid $100 an hour as a face-saving way of helping that family. Or maybe brother-in-law works for free because of the stupid thing that he's trying to make up for. If the seller mismanaged the asset, that does not mean the property is bad. In fact, seller's mismanagement is an example of right thing wrong with a property. Mismanagement is easy to fix. So, the seller's income and expenses or management choices don't determine the buyer's choices or results.

Here is another reason to have a great broker on your team. The expert can recognize the nonsense numbers (no vacancy or expenses that are out of line). Mediocre agents may not know what typical insurance or utility costs are, or they may not be able to identify the costs that are omitted. A pro knows what to look for; he or she has a BS detector. On the worksheet, I disregard the listing broker's fluff and instead calculated NOI using the criteria the loan underwriter will use. In other words, I aim to filter out the seller's and listing broker's errors.

Year Built—newer assets tend to be worth more than older ones. Style, building codes, and wear and tear all affect value.

Unit Mix tells the number of studio apartments, one, two, and three bedrooms. The importance of the mix will vary by market. In San Diego, fewer than 10% of apartments have three bedrooms, so three bedrooms push the value up. But that isn't true in many other markets. Your broker will help you understand this characteristic and everything else on the list.

Suggested Offer is the column on the far right. The figure represents my professional judgment. I consider the building, the area, and the market, as well as my client's goals and preferences.

What You Do with It

This prioritizing tool can help you zero in on the higher probability options from the blizzard of numbers. Human beings aren't naturally good at making decisions when there are many choices. Here's how Barry Schwartz, a psychology professor at Swarthmore, describes it:

> . . . studies have confirmed this result that more choice is not always better. As the variety of snacks, soft drinks, and beers offered at convenience stores increases, for instance, sales volume and customer satisfaction decrease. Moreover, as the number of retirement investment options available to employees increases, the chance that they will choose any decreases. These studies and others have shown not only that excessive choice can produce "choice paralysis," but also that it can reduce people's satisfaction with their decisions, even if they made good ones.

I want our clients to make wise decisions and feel good about them. There are essentially two ways to avoid choice paralysis. One way is to reduce the number of options, usually to four or fewer. The other way is to create a process to make it easier to consider the relevant options and make a wise choice among them. The spreadsheet does both.

First, we highlight which properties are better on certain criteria. With color coding or circling, we can highlight that properties 1, 5, and 6 have low List Price per square foot and that properties 1, 5, and 7 have superior Cap Rates. For each key criterion, we usually highlight approximately about a third of the properties that are the best value or most desirable according to at least one metric. Then we look at the next feature and note which roughly one-third of the properties are most attractive according to that measurement. We continue until each metric has been considered.

Properties that are superior in three or four categories are more likely to be a superior investment than properties that score well in only one or two categories. The investor can still write offers on other properties. This tool focuses attention to the few opportunities that are most likely to bring success. The sorting mechanism also provides guidance about how hard to bargain. If we find a screaming winner, we might write a full-price offer or maybe even higher. A property that just barely makes the finalist list might get a lower offer.

On the example page you see, we chose the best third based on a goal of building wealth. This process could be used with clients who have different goals. If the investor preferred ease of management or wanted to buy and never sell, then other sorting criteria would help identify the most likely candidates.

The best third on each criterion are the best third of the subset of properties on the sheet only. There may be 100 other assets for sale. Part of our value as brokers is finding and sorting options. Most properties are listed and known to many brokers; some may not be officially on the market. Next month another buyer may consider a similar market or have different capital. Prices adjust. The tool simply nudges investors toward writing smart offers on several logical possibilities that my clients will go and see. After that, we talk about the options, and their feedback enables me to educate them about what the marketplace values and why.

This simple chart focuses attention and then provokes intelligent discussion. We don't talk about the color of exterior paint. Instead we talk about comparative value of neighborhoods and relative weight of unit mix versus price or age or some other measure. As a guide, my assignment is to help you move closer to your goal. When a client does not write offers, either the broker or the principal is wasting time, and they are fooling themselves.

The tool focuses our discussion on the best options. Client feedback enables me to serve them well. Together we become a better team.

The Outcome

Our goal is to select several properties to write intelligent offers on. Intelligent offers are likely to bring some counteroffers. The process educates clients about market reality. Many people learn better when they see the preferred building go to someone who moved faster or who wrote higher offers.

Better informed clients are wiser clients. Learning is an important result of this process. "Failing forward" is something that winners advocate. "Make new and better mistakes" also describes growing. The sequence of buying apartments differs from buying a home. The next chapter outlines what precedes the offer, through due diligence, final price adjustment, signing loan documents, and closing.

Successful Buying

"He who will not risk cannot win."
~ John Paul Jones

"Nothing is more difficult, and therefore more precious,
than to be able to decide."
~ Napoleon

"There is a tide in the affairs of men, which, taken at the flood,
leads on to fortune; omitted, all the voyage of their life is bound
in the shallows and in miseries; and we must take the current
when it serves, or lose our ventures."
~ Shakespeare

"Insanity is doing the same thing over and over
and expecting a different result."
*(That quote has been attributed to Albert Einstein, Mark Twain,
and Ben Franklin. Regardless of who originated it, it's true.)*

TOO MANY APARTMENT BROKERS AND INVESTORS work with one property per client at a time. That system delivers poor results. Many other buyers were also seeking that same "best property." Since only one could get the property, all the rest had to start the process over. So I improved our process.

We began making offers on several properties, not just one asset. It doesn't matter that we will miss on several because when our client closes, that's a win. Your success is closing on the best available option; the ones you don't buy do not matter. I can't stress this enough. The only properties that will help you build wealth and leave a legacy are the ones you buy, improve, and sell. No property that you do not buy will help you build wealth. But what about regret?

In my decades of brokerage experience, I'm unaware of any of my clients who believe they made a mistake by paying a quarter of a percent too much. Alternatively, I know more than 50 investors who regret not paying just a little bit more to capture the deal they missed.

In the last chapter, you learned about our prioritizing system and how it helps you identify your best options from all available properties. Few brokers use a process like it. This chapter introduces a buying process that turned many of my clients into millionaires and deca-millionaires. These tactics may be new to your broker, so invite him or her to read this chapter. Experience proves it is a superior tool for buyers and their broker. Here's how I explain the process to a client:

> There are no perfect properties. Your goal is to purchase the best property from among the available imperfect options. We will achieve your wealth-building goal by multitasking. An engineer might say we will work in parallel instead of in series.
>
> Let's make many intelligent offers on properties more likely to build legacy wealth. Some sellers will reject our offers; others will give an unmotivated counteroffer. Some buildings may be under contract before the seller receives our offer. Some sellers will counter

our offer and then, after some counteroffers, we may get two or three under contract. We'll inspect them and, after reviewing all relevant information, you'll pick the one that, by definition, you think is the best in the marketplace.

Pardon me for stating the obvious. Finding a mate is different from buying the best income property. The best way to find a mate is different from the best way to find a terrific property. My multiple offer system is more effective for wealth building.

- You'll learn why the multiple offers strategy works and how the Offer Dashboard tracks the options;
- You'll understand why writing backup offers is a key part of the strategy and how to make intelligent offers and negotiate to close; and
- You'll grasp how to avoid the one thing that can absolutely prevent you from building the legacy wealth you want.

How Apartment Investing Is Not Like Making a Marriage Proposal

Some people act as if writing an offer is the same as proposing marriage. They don't want to make any forward motion until they are sure it's a perfect match. The better analogy is that writing an offer is like going on a coffee date. If you see something you like, you move a half step closer. When and if what you see no longer appears like a good match, you gracefully exit.

Writing multiple offers saves time in discovering which sellers are most motivated and which available properties are the best fits. Think speed dating but with no stress. We dramatically improve the odds of acquiring an excellent property.

The Logic and Practice of Multiple Offers

After handling more than 3,000 offers, I'm convinced that a multiple-offer strategy is the most effective way to build legacy wealth. It's similar to what MBAs, math geeks, and "quants" call a queueing problem or toll-bridge problem.

For a toll bridge, the speed that cars get onto the bridge is a function of how fast they can clear the toll booths. Faster access can happen by reducing the time to get through a toll booth, or increasing the number of toll booths or both. Here's how that works in apartment investing.

Most offers aren't accepted; and some percentage, maybe 20–35% of accepted offers don't close, usually because the operating history or inspection causes the buyer to decline to continue. Sometimes the buyer asks for a bigger concession than the seller will give. If you're making one offer at a time, you must restart whenever your escrow fails. Buyers don't know and can't control property condition or the seller's response to repair requests.

But multiple offers enable us to get double or triple or better use of the same time. Tech geeks often refer to the OODA Loop (Observe-Orient-Decide-Act Loop) developed by Colonel John Boyd to help fighter pilots make decisions faster than their opponents. The multiple-offer strategy helps you do the same thing: Make decisions faster than other investors. The faster you act, the more chances at bat, and the better your odds of capturing a property that meets your objectives.

If an offer isn't accepted or if an accepted offer doesn't close, you still have other offers working. You're almost certain to have the opportunity to close on a superior wealth building property. Not only that, but you're more likely to get the available property that's the best fit for you.

By now you may be tired of hearing me say that "there is no perfect property," but that truth is key to a multiple-offers strategy. Every apartment-investing opportunity will be different—unique cluster of imperfections. When you make multiple offers, the building you close on will have the best set of fixable imperfections available, the ones that fit the investor, landlord, and human being that you want to be.

Sellers obtain relatively prompt feedback from multiple buyers. If the price is too high, then no one writes an offer. If multiple buyers stopped near the same price or object to identical issue, the seller can learn from that. In effect the seller gains feedback as they try to sell simultaneously to multiple buyers.

A multiple offer strategy evens the odds. Multiple sellers responding to the same buyer's offer. Buyer quickly gains feedback. Instead of waiting for one reluctant seller to move forward, the buyer can learn from the seller to respond promptly and move forward even if one seller never responds. With the multiple-offer strategy, the buyer progresses rapidly even if one seller responds late or never responds.

The two big upsides to the multiple-offer strategy are increased speed to close and wider choice of properties. There's small downside for a lazy broker. Most of the offers won't close. Amazingly, some brokers want big bucks without having to do excellent work. My Offer Dashboard summarizes the current info on each available option.

The Offer Dashboard—the Force Multiplier

Tracking the ever-changing status of available options is tedious. Think of being able to bet on horses a quarter of the way or halfway or three quarters of the way around the track. You need the current relative status to know which few properties seem best with current information. It simplifies comparison of the most critical information about current targets. As properties drop out or are added, the dashboard enables you and your broker to quickly assess where each one ranks. A version of the dashboard is on the next page.

The top two rows identify the property by address and location. Below that is "Offer Status." In this example, we're part way through the process. We wrote offers on several properties, but we don't know yet which ones we'll pay for inspection on. We have one accepted offer, and there's one where we've sent a contract to the investor for their electronic signature. There are three properties where we have not yet made an offer. For most of the properties, we're somewhere between "We ought to look at this" and "We can buy it if we want it."

As we go through the offer process, the dashboard reminds us of the relative position of each opportunity. We might say, "Okay, this first property is adequate, and there's nothing left to do to it. This second building may use half the rehab money to correct roof and sewer, which doesn't raise rents. On this third one, anything we do is going to improve it. Every dollar we spend will create more value."

Today's cash flow has value; but future cash flow is far more important. The dashboard focuses us on the future potential. It helps us estimate which asset will produce best cash flow after renovation. It encourages making intelligent estimates of future results. If we spent $10K, or some other appropriate amount for rehab, what kind of rent might this property generate?

Did I mention that building wealth is hard? Everything worthwhile you ever did was hard. Thinking is hard. Thinking well is hard. You'll be wrong a lot. However, you're not doing brain surgery. You only need to win by an inch, not by a mile. Your pretty good guess is probably better than your competitor who does not even try to estimate future outcomes.

Our "guesstimates" can be helpful during negotiation when we hit a speed bump. The dashboard helps us calibrate the ultimate investment value. In other words, it helps us decide whether to push forward in a negotiation or move on to a different property.

My clients love the Offer Dashboard's power. Most of them have a day job and a family and life's usual challenges. If I'm lucky, I get three hours of their mind a week. The Offer Dashboard concentrates our attention quickly on important issues and facilitates efficient conversations about what we should do. Here's a detailed description of the items on the Offer Dashboard.

The **List Price** is what the seller selected. Below it is the **Target Price**, which is my professional judgment about a realistic target. This is where your broker's experience and relationships come into play. Sometimes the Target Price is a calculated guess based on what I know about the building and the area and the market. Sometimes that guess is enhanced because the

OFFER DASHBOARD - BOB BUYER						
Address	Apple St San Diego	Berry St San Diego	Orange St San Diego	Pear Ave San Diego	Grape St San Diego	Lemon St San Diego
Offer Status		Submitted offer at $800K		$1.35 Offer - waiting for response		Buyer Counter 1 - $1.26 sent
List Price	$1,800,000	$945,000	$2,350,000	$1,570,000	$2,990,000	$1,385,000
Target Price	**$1,650,000**	**$879,000**	**$2,200,000**	**$1,450,000**	**$2,850,000**	**$1,290,000**
# of Units	9	6	14	6	20	8
% 2 bedrooms or more	44%	83%	100%	100%	10%	100%
GSI	$132,340	$74,400	$165,000	$103,800	$231,060	$113,400
Collections after 4% vacancy	$126,950	$71,424	$158,400	$99,648	$221,818	$108,864
Expenses:						
Taxes (1.05% rate)	$16,275	$9,230	$22,050	$14,175	$27,825	$13,230
Other expenses $3K (+/-)/unit	$27,000	$18,000	$44,800	$19,200	$56,000	$25,600
*Under 40% 2 bdrms $2,800/unit *Between 40–60% 2 bdrms $3,000/unit *Over 60% 2 bdrms $3,200/unit						
Total Expense	$43,275	$27,230	$66,850	$33,375	$83,825	$38,830
NOI	$83,675	$44,194	$91,550	$66,273	$137,993	$70,034
Annual Mortgage Payment	$68,078	$36,637	$76,414	$55,574	$111,957	$53,768
Rate 3.75%/amortization 30						
Cash Flow Year 1	$15,597	$7,557	$15,136	$10,699	$26,036	$16,266
Loan Pay Down	$22,525	$12,122	$25,283	$18,388	$37,043	$17,790
First Year Benefit	$38,122	$21,121	$40,419	$29,087	$63,079	$34,056
Cash Flow Year 2**	$20,891	$10,533	$21,736	$14,851	$35,278	$20,802
(After upgrades + 7% rent increase)						
Loan	$1,225,000	$659,250	$1,375,000	$1,000,000	$2,093,000	$967,500
Down Payment*	$425,000	$219,750	$825,000	$450,000	$757,000	$322,500
Rehab	$72,000	$72,000	$35,000	$42,000	$42,000	$80,000
Total Cash In	$459,500	$291,750	$860,000	$492,000	$799,000	$402,500
Estimated Cash on Cash Year 2	3.5%	2.4%	2.3%	2.6%	4.0%	3.7%
*In effect, this assumes rehab money will come from other money not part of the 1031 proceeds.						
$6K/unit extra rehab	$54,000	$36,000	$84,000	$36,000	$120,000	$48,000
Cash flow year 2	$37,344	$19,729	$42,130	$27,681	$63,837	$34,818
Total benefit year 2	$59,869	$31,851	$67,413	$46,069	$100,880	$52,608

listing broker has accidentally or deliberately revealed his client's motivation or something about property condition or because a little birdie told me something else. Nice guys get tips from a host of industry professionals—people you would not think of.

Last week an unbiased industry expert told me about a highly desirable property that might be available, even though it was not officially on the market. Recently an appraiser I've helped in dozens of ways over the years helped me determine rent levels and renovation results for a property we were considering.

Recently, I was dealing with a known scoundrel I'll call Smythe. I was trying to decide whether to spend our limited hours trying to salvage a transaction with Smythe or drop it and concentrate on something that would be more likely to close. I had a chance conversation with someone who had worked for Smythe, and who shared some of Smythe's tactics with me. It was enough to convince us to abandon the transaction and move on to something less dangerous and more likely to be profitable for my client.

Some folks see the "little birdies" as unimportant people. Yet scores of honorable people are important to closing escrows or operating rentals. Most don't earn $100K, but they deserve respect. Occasionally a "little birdie" is a major player returning a favor or trying to penalize a jerk. I'm always grateful for any ethical advantage, and I never reveal my sources. Now, let's return to the dashboard.

We list **# of Units** and **% 2 bedrooms or more** as information. In San Diego, units with two bedrooms or more add value. That may or may not be true where you are, but your broker will be able to suggest other value-adding features that you should be aware of.

GSI stands for Gross Scheduled Income. GSI is the highest potential income at today's rates if you get all the rents from all the units all the time, 100% occupancy, and perfect rent payment. That's helpful to know, but it won't happen in real life. That's why we include **GOI** (Gross Operating

Income) to estimate the money you will receive from tenants. I estimate local vacancy and credit loss. Your broker will know your market's rates.

Expenses are the amount you are likely to spend to operate the property. Many listing brokers will claim that a property will require an unrealistically low amount to operate. My estimates are based on how banks underwrite properties. Your broker should provide a realistic figure. I show the figures so my investors understand the thinking and the assumptions. **Total Expenses** include property taxes and other operating expenses.

NOI stands for Net Operating Income, and it's your cash flow before the mortgage payment. Here's the arithmetic for the far-left property on the dashboard:

GOI	$126,950
Minus: Property taxes Operating expenses	– $16,275 – $27,000
Equals NOI	= $83.675

California property taxes are just over 1% of purchase price, and once the tax amount is established, it can only increase by 2% annually.

Cash Flow Yr 1 is the amount of cash you'll have at the end of the first year, if you don't do anything to increase rents. To get it, subtract the **Mortgage Payment** from NOI. Loan Paydown is the principal reduction in that first year. When we add that to your cash flow, we get the **First Year Benefit.**

Below that is **Cash Flow Yr 2**. Your market will have a different amount of expected rental increase after renovations. The figure there is based on San Diego's 7% increase in the rental income that's listed as GSI. You'll find strategies for increasing rents and cash flow in the Renovation Budgets and Strategies chapter.

The next four rows show where the money will come from to buy the building and do the renovations. The **Loan** is the amount the investor will borrow. The investor will put up the **Down Payment** amount and the

Rehab Budget, which together are the **Total Cash In** that the investor needs to have. You can change the mix of Down Payment and Rehab Budget so you have more or less money available for rehab. You'll find more on this in the Renovation Budgets and Strategies chapter.

The bottom row on the dashboard is **Estimated Cash on Cash Year 2.** It's the cash flow for Year 2 divided by the amount you had to spend to make that happen (Total Cash In).

The Offer Dashboard tracks the status of offers as we implement our multiple-offer strategy. The reason to write backup offers is to increase your wealth-building progress.

It Isn't Just Crunching Numbers

Buying is not just number crunching that can be done by Mr. Spock. Real people live in these apartments, so things like floor plans matter.

Some floor plans are spectacular. A few are abysmal. Most, maybe 70%, are in the middle—acceptable, but not inspired. If you stumble onto a great floor plan, with little waste and good flow, rejoice and be willing to pay slightly more.

If the apartment is chopped up or weird, having to enter one bedroom though another, be careful and consider declining the property. Sometimes it can be cost effective to buy at a big enough discount to demolish and reconfigure some walls. If the problem can't be solved cost effectively, then the asset may be one with the wrong things wrong with it.

Why Writing Backup Offers Is a Key Part of the Strategy

Backup offers take time and energy and have low success probability. Over my career, about 20% of all my buy-side closings were after the first deal failed.

Many brokers prefer higher pay per hour. Respectfully, my motivation is different; my calling is to help my clients win. California is among the many states that impose fiduciary responsibility on real estate licensees. Fiduciary responsibility means putting the client's interest ahead of the broker's interest.

There are two more layers of truth. When my clients win, they become wealthier, often do more business, and often refer more clients. It is another example of helping people get what they want and being well rewarded. Besides all that, *I love it when we win!* When my clients win, my entire team wins!

Let's be clear why backup offers help the buyer. Remember that many escrows fail. When an escrow fails, the listing broker wants to get the asset into escrow again. If only one buyer has written a sensible backup offer, then that broker is likely to get the first call and perhaps the opportunity to capture the property. But if there are no back-up offers, then many brokers or perhaps the full market will be notified. So the broker and buyer team with a sensible backup offer often gets a head start.

Intelligent Offers

An intelligent offer has better than a 50% chance of being countered. Writing offers that won't be countered wastes time and credibility. We write offers to obtain counters and learn more about the seller's motivation and the property.

Every used apartment building is unique, and the seller will choose only one buyer for the building. He or she may have multiple offers; but in the end, there will be only one buyer. The challenge for you and your broker is to package yourself as a buyer who is capable, realistic, and nimble. Your intelligent offer increases your odds of winning.

Negotiating to Close

In every market, there is a way for rich strangers to show enough strength to be taken seriously and to gradually reveal more confidential information to each other. Every market has slightly different practices. Your excellent broker will guide you through the local market and customs.

Most offers will generate counteroffers, but sometimes you will get no response or the seller makes a trivial price reduction. When that happens, we often end our pursuit of that property and move on.

When you receive a reasonable counteroffer, you begin a business dance with the seller. It may take from two to five counteroffers before the buyer and seller reach agreement.

More Power Is Available When the Capital Justifies It

This volume is written for investors with, say, $200K to $5 million in equity to place. Bigger chunks of money merit more intense analysis. CCIMs and other effective professionals can help their clients run projections for 5, 10, or 20 years. You can model the impact of various interest rates, ending cap rates, and various income and expense growth paths. I have whiled away hundreds of hours in such intellectual speculation. However—my crystal ball is cracked. You or your broker can run projections till the cows come home. Most experts have an abysmal record of forecasting. Candidly, not even my decamillionaire clients run the sophisticated analysis I can do. The marketplace has humbled us by doing something different than what the model says.

If you enjoy the hobby of electronic "what if," good for you. Simply remember that the market does not know or care what your model says. Your tenants will respond to how you treat them. The worldwide interest rate does not care about you or the state you're in. A 1% rate swing will have a bigger effect on your exit sales price than whether the property's income rose 1% slower or faster than your projections.

There are fancier and more powerful projection tools. However, extra computing power does not guarantee you a better result.

A Bias for Action and the Propensity to Pounce

Apartment investing can be a fast-moving sport. One reason it's smart to define your values up front is that you won't lose time having to decide what's important to you every time you want to buy an investment property. Knowing your target and your capacity enables you to more quickly buy when the right property becomes available.

Multiple offers give buyers the option, but not the obligation, to buy.

Next, you perform the due diligence and negotiating process. At the end of that process you may have two or three properties that will build your legacy wealth. Then you have to decide and close. Winners have a bias for action to start the process, to do the analysis, to negotiate, and to keep moving forward to close. That's what great investors do.

Great Investors Have the Propensity to Pounce

Sometimes a few days' delay in submitting an offer doesn't matter. Sometimes you'll get a second chance, but you can't count on that.

Just remember that, in commercial investing, the buyer conducts due diligence after the seller has accepted an offer. Investors who want to "be sure" before writing an offer frequently lose out to others who think the opportunity looks good enough to tie up the property and then investigate. **Only the investor who puts the property under contract** has enough time to research it. All others can only hope they get another chance to buy it. Most of the time there is no second chance.

A few months ago, one of our smart clients lost out on a superior opportunity. They tried to do too much due diligence before writing an offer. They didn't want to "waste" $1.5K on an inspection report. While the client was investigating, another buyer submitted an offer. After the inspection, the competitor asked for an outrageous discount. If our buyer had submitted an offer, the seller might have talked to us, but that didn't happen.

The seller felt time pressure and, instead of exploring the option with our strong, well-qualified buyer, simply caved in to the buyer who was at the table. If our buyer had written the offer first and then done due diligence, then the other competitor would have never inspected the property, much less bought it for less than our buyers were willing to pay. If our buyers had "gambled" the $1.5K on an inspection report, they would probably have gotten a deal that was a newer unit in a better location and at least a $10K better value than their next best option.

Investment property is different from new cars or new suits. You can't order another just like the one you missed, because every building is unique. Due-diligence costs are trivial in comparison to missing the best deal of the year. Also, custom-order cars take longer and always cost full retail.

Often the best options are captured when an investor decides quickly. You or your broker may learn of a price reduction or rent increase or increased seller motivation or some other important fact. Trusted, active brokers routinely learn such facts that most agents never learn. When that happens, you have two choices. You can pounce or not.

The best investors pounce.

Pouncing enables you to write offers and put properties into escrow. A vital function, confirming that property is acceptable through a due diligence process, is covered in Appendix C, Due Diligence.

Escrow is opened after you have an agreement on price and terms, and that's when the due-diligence process begins. You will put up some earnest money; you and the seller will share confidential information with each other. You'll demonstrate that you have enough cash or other liquidity for the down payment and a lender who is likely to finance the property. The seller will share financial information—the property's income and expenses, contracts with vendors, and tenant leases—and grant the buyer access to talk to residents and to inspect the asset—all the units, plumbing, roof, foundation, and other building systems.

The property inspection has three major goals:

- To avoid disaster
- To provide negotiating strength
- To act as a budgeting and operating tool

Pardon me as I fuss about a common report format. Too often I see a report that mentions that:

- X might be a problem, consult with a contractor.

- Y might be a problem, consult with a contractor.

- Z might be a problem, consult with a contractor.

That type of report is almost useless. In income properties, the buyer does *not* have the ability to come back for a second, third, or fourth inspection. If the inspector can't interpret or advise, then what value does the inspector provide?

Anyway, let's get back to the value that a superb inspector can deliver.

First, the inspection is cost-effective insurance. The inspector is not there to find trivia like reverse polarity in an electrical outlet. Instead, you hire the inspector to find the $10K problems that you and the broker might not understand. If the inspector warns of substantial flaws, that's terrific; you can make an informed decision.

An excellent inspection frequently reveals things about the building that not even the seller or the listing agent knows. You and your broker can use the inspection report to negotiate a discount. Often, a competent broker using a thorough inspection report can obtain concessions that will be greater than the cost of the inspector's report.

When people buy homes, some buyers expect the seller to fix most things mentioned in the inspection report. When you buy a used apartment building, you're buying an income stream, not a model home. The property only needs to be in safe and habitable condition.

The interior inspection will show that property is used and was built to an earlier building code. One reason for the report is to reveal whether condition matches reasonable expectations, given what can be reasonably expected for a property of its vintage in that neighborhood, and given what can be seen from the outside. If the inside is a terrible disappointment, the buyer may cancel the escrow, obtain a refund of his earnest money, and run screaming in the other direction. Alternatively, the buyer might ask for a large discount.

If the interior is near reasonable expectations, then the transaction probably goes forward. It's prudent to hire a top-notch building inspector for an expert opinion. Your broker should be able to point you to the top inspectors in your area.

Besides arranging for the physical building inspection, you should do other things during the due-diligence period. They include ensuring that the title is clean or will be clean by the close of escrow, and determining if the books and records will support the loan specified in the offer. Be sure to check Appendix C, Due Diligence, for more details.

Perhaps 20–30% of escrows fail because of what is learned during the due-diligence process. Sometimes the listing broker or seller did not accurately understand or appropriately disclose material facts. Sometimes buyers or their brokers have unrealistic assumptions. Sometimes buyer and seller can't agree on what is an appropriate adjustment for the asset's true condition. Occasionally, a buyer won't be able to arrange financing. If any of those things happen, we go back to the offer dashboard and decide on our next steps.

That's my multiple-offer strategy. You've learned how and why it works, and you've been exposed to my Offer Dashboard for keeping track of the offers. The process works, but you must avoid one tragic mistake that too many investors make: They wait too long.

In this chapter, you learned about my multiple-offer system for purchasing investment property. When you become a property owner, you start another adventure. And that's what we'll cover in the next chapter.

Successful Operating

"Success is relative: it's what we can make of the mess
we've made of things."
~ T.S. Eliot

"Part of wisdom is the art of knowing what to overlook."
~ Paraphrase of William James

"There are two things needed in these days: rich men to find out how
poor men live; and second, for poor men to know how rich men work."
~ Edward Atkinson

Pride of ownership is great, but most of our clients achieve their
wealth-building goals by thinking about how to develop the *potential* of
property. When you purchase your first building, you enter the world of
landlording, and you have many choices about how to build wealth and
legacy. Your desired legacy should drive all your choices. This chapter is
about your important rental-ownership decisions.

You'll discover what makes a good landlord and why two kinds of people should never be landlords. You'll learn how to decide how to handle management and maintenance, including how to set rents and how to add value to your property. My generation of ownership and brokerage experience will provide some cautions based on expensive life lessons.

In order to lead a life worth imitating, most of us need to grow beyond who we are now. You and I are not better than the people we deal with. In many situations, you may be the wealthiest or the wisest person in the room. Some of your residents and people who serve your residents will have less income or less education or maybe less emotional intelligence. Some folks are wounded, and some of those wounds are self-inflected. It is easy to be nice to nice people. Character is shown in dealing with difficult people and in bad situations.

Great people are known by the way they treat weak people. Everyone you want to influence notices how you deal with others. Live the stories you want people to tell about you.

As a landlord, you will impact many people whom you would never encounter otherwise. Rental owners have more and deeper contact with renters than investors who only own stocks and bonds. To wrap up this chapter, I'll share two ways that landlording can build your legacy. But first, let's consider what it takes to be a good landlord.

Landlords: Good and Bad

Good landlords provide clean, safe, and functional housing for their tenants. Good landlords understand their tenants as people, not revenue sources, and show that compassionate perspective by their actions.

Good landlords have clear "house rules," and they are firm, fair, and consistent in enforcing those rules. Good landlords respect tenant privacy, listen to complaints and suggestions, and make repairs properly and promptly.

Good landlords also increase their property's value. The best landlords learn how to obtain the best rent increase for the lowest cost: That creates value for the rental owner and for your residents. Renters may like you more after you make the property better for them. When you improve their rental home, you can raise the rent, and they pay you more.

Just about anyone can learn how to be a good landlord, and anyone with enough money can buy a building and become a landlord. But there are two kinds of people I believe should not become landlords, because they will never be good ones.

If I'm polite, may I be direct? If you're a bigot, please don't become a landlord. Not all tenants will look like you, cook like you, vote like you, or have your spiritual worldview. In the United States, fair housing laws prohibit discrimination based on race, religion, or other factors. If you can't tolerate people who are different from you, then make your life and theirs easier; invest in stocks, bonds, or commodities. Federal law is potent, and bigotry makes rental ownership just too hard for all concerned.

Don't be a slumlord. Uninformed people might think a slumlord as any landlord who rents to poor people. What differentiates a landlord and a slumlord is the way they act. Both rent real estate to people, usually folks with less income and lower net worth.

It's the owner's actions, not the residents' income, that define whether the owner is a slumlord. Slumlords exploit their tenants, put tenants' health and safety at risk, and don't perform necessary maintenance. That's bad ethics. Perhaps in the short run it might seem slumlords have some economic gain, but slumlording won't put you on the escalator to build legacy wealth, because you will not increase the value of your property.

In contrast, wise owners respect tenants and improve the property. They earn solid economic benefits. Wise landlords understand that the next buyer will pay more for an asset with higher income and lower costs. Smart landlords build wealth *before* they sell; then they trade up and repeat the process.

You'll decide what kind of good landlord you want to be, based on your strengths and weaknesses and the legacy you want to leave. You'll decide who will handle management and maintenance, how you will set rents, and how you will boost your property's value. Let's consider management and maintenance first.

Decisions about Management and Maintenance

Rental ownership isn't rocket science. If you apply yourself, you can almost certainly learn what you need to know. Plenty of courses, books, and articles will help you learn how to do a good job. For about 100 years, the Southern California Rental Housing Association, formerly San Diego County Apartment Association, has excelled at helping owners become better landlords. They teach the basics, help owners keep up with changes in laws and regulations, and provide opportunities to learn from other landlords. There's probably an apartment owners' association near you.

People pleasers may have difficulty being landlords. Some residents who are unrelated to you will wish that you would rent to them for half price. They will ask for concessions and special treatment. After all, in their minds, you're rich and they are not, so you "owe" them something. People pleasers are likely to say "yes" to those requests and, very soon, other tenants learn that they will get special treatment if they ask. As I said earlier, if you're a people pleaser, you should probably avoid the face-to-face part of rental ownership.

Paul and Betty used the "family farm" model of landlording. They did the management and most of the maintenance themselves, and that system helped them build wealth faster than if they had hired others to do some of the work. That isn't the right choice for everyone. Your choice of whether to hire management and maintenance or do it yourself comes down to answers to three basic questions.

Does it make economic sense to hire management and maintenance?

Compare your hourly rate with the hourly rate you'll pay for someone else to do the work. I've known two janitors who were also successful landlords.

It probably makes sense for janitors who are landlords to do as much themselves as possible, but it makes no economic sense for neurosurgeons or top-notch attorneys to do the maintenance work themselves.

What about your strengths and weaknesses?

Identify your strengths and weakness, the things you don't enjoy doing, and the types of situations you find especially stressful. If you're a people pleaser, or if seeing how your tenants live upsets you, avoid the face-to-face parts of property management. If you're not sure which end of a hammer to hold, don't even think about doing maintenance yourself.

If you're great with tools and can fix just about anything, you still may not want to do it at your rental property. If you don't enjoy the work, you might put it off; but then both tenant relations and maintenance will suffer.

What's the right choice for your legacy?

Here are three perspectives on legacy in relation to management and maintenance.

First, some clients decided that part of their legacy was to be a person who helped less fortunate people. They understood rental ownership as a way to do that on a day-to-day basis.

Second, some investors have amazing mechanical skills. They love fixing things and making the property safer and more efficient. Maximizing income or net worth isn't of major importance to them. Their chosen legacy is to routinely improve their properties.

Third, for other landlords, the main goal is to build wealth that they will bequeath to their children and charities. They choose options based on what will be best for improving the cash flow and property value.

Some landlords decide based on more than one of the previous questions. One contractor chose to do the high dollar jobs in his specialty, and those tasks that he could do for less than a third of a service call. He hired others to make other repairs and improvements, and he retained a management company for everything else.

Since this book is about building legacy wealth, consider this suggestion: Unless you have a drive or calling to repair used buildings or talk to your tenants weekly, simply delegate tasks that others can do better or more cost effectively. Your broker can guide you to quality firms.

Decisions about Setting Rents

In most places, the market sets the upper limit on rents. In San Diego, for example, it isn't uncommon to see essentially the same apartment rented for $900, $1,000, and $1,100, and most of the tenants won't know what the other tenants are paying. Thus, you have more flexibility than most people realize. That is part of why I call it face-to-face capitalism. If you don't want to deal with the hassle and expense of tenant turnover, you can set your rent at the low end of the market. On the other hand, you can choose to maximize value by setting the rent higher and upgrading your building.

It is permissible within Federal fair housing laws to charge different rates for different units rented at various times, but it is not permissible to discriminate against protected classes. So it is permissible to discriminate between smokers and nonsmokers, or between left-handed and right-handed people, because those are not "protected classes." Protected classes are defined by law. The current laws say that discrimination based on a tenant's race, religion, national origin, or sexual orientation is illegal.

You may visit your competition to determine what rents they charge and learn how a potential renter would compare your rental to that of your neighbor. Gaining this market intelligence is called shopping the competition. Those actions are examples of face-to-face capitalism. If you don't talk to residents, then your property manager does it for you. But as a landlord, your decisions affect people directly. It is different from looking at stock prices on a computer screen. Landlording offers you many options for building your legacy. Choose your best fit.

Decisions about Adding Value to Your Property

You have many options about improving your property's value. You'll find a full menu of options and a description of renovation strategies in the Renovation Budgets and Strategies chapter. Your property manager, your broker, and others who know about tenant preferences can help you decide what to do and, more importantly, what not to do. Ask renters whose judgment you trust: "If your landlord was going to renovate your apartment and your rent was going up 5%, would you rather have X or Y?"

Work the way the eye doctor works when examining your eyes. They install two lenses and then ask you. "Which is better: 1 or 2?" Then the doctor replaces the inferior lens with a different lens and asks the question again. The process is repeated until the best choices are clear. Step by step, you figure out which lens strength is appropriate. Follow a similar process when you're deciding what renovations to make. Steadily you will learn what your target residents value. Let them show and tell you what they will pay for. You don't want to spend twice as much as needed to earn the same rent increase.

It's worth investing more than a day to calibrate how much you'll have to spend to achieve the target rents. You may dress down one day and shop the competition. What features do they have, and what did they skip? Then talk with your ideal or target renters: Would you prefer A or B? This market intelligence enables you to add value for residents and wisely build your own wealth as well. Fair housing prohibits discriminating against protected classes: race, religion, national origin, etc. It is permissible to make your property more appealing to pet owners, kayakers, left-handed people, or people who want to be near people in a Meetup group.

Making Wise Rental Ownership Choices

Landlording offers the opportunity to build the legacy wealth you want, but there are many moving parts. As the property owner, you will decide who will manage the building and do the maintenance. You'll determine the rents. You'll decide what renovations are appropriate. All those choices have trade-offs. I have been a landlord for over 30 years, and for more than a generation I have guided hundreds of other rental owners. Millionaire clients have valued these ideas.

If your goal is to build legacy wealth, remember that goal

Stephen Covey counsels us to **begin with the end in mind**. The best landlords learn how to obtain the best rent increase for the lowest cost and, thus create maximum value. I've outlined some options in the Renovation Budgets and Strategies chapter.

Your property can produce higher cash flow in multiple ways. The more desirable the property is, the higher the rents and the lower the vacancy rate. Wise material choices can mean longer life and lower maintenance costs. Some choices will be made because of the *Wow!* factor. Manufacturers, merchants, and people who design menus all consider the perceived value from the customer's perspective, as well as the cost to the business. You're in that game now; play it well.

Envision your ideal resident . . . in a fair housing way

Upgrade and renovate based on the budget and taste of the folks you aspire to rent to. *Do not* upgrade and renovate based on your personal taste and what pleases you and your family.

In our county, an outrageously successful investor specialized in working-class neighborhoods. After he understood his target renter, whenever he bought a building, he would take out the garbage disposals and on turnover throw away the carpet and install tile. His target market was first-generation Americans who didn't grow up with garbage disposals and did not own vacuum cleaners. He purchased the stoves and installed the countertops and kitchen cabinets his tenants were comfortable with. If they would not pay for an upgrade, then it was a waste to buy those improvements. He understood and complied with fair housing practices. He concentrated on delivering the best value according to his tenants' taste and budget.

Manage your emotions

Some people feel guilty that they have more money and resources than their tenants have. If thoughts like that gnaw at you, remember this: It isn't your fault. Let's consider some realities.

Many people rent between leaving their parents' home and before buying their own home. Other people will always be renters because either they made some unwise choices or they encountered some bad luck. Perhaps they fell in love with someone who committed a felony. Addiction and divorce snag millions. Many things can cause people to remain tenants instead of becoming homeowners. You didn't cause any of that.

Here's another economic reality. Everyone must live somewhere. Your best investment opportunities may be in low-income zip codes. Those folks face some hard choices every day, and those choices define how they live. It's probably very different from how you live, and it may make you uncomfortable to know that some people live that way. If that's true, then the face-to-face part of rental ownership is probably not for you.

Be clear about your legacy objective

Who matters more to you, your grandkids or your residents?

There are several right answers to the legacy question. Some wonderful landlords have not raised the rent in 20 years. Their tenants love them. The owner knows they are subsidizing their tenants. That's a completely ethical and honorable choice.

Some landladies I serve are more interested in building legacy for the grandkids. These landladies charge market rate for their rentals. Sometimes long-standing residents leave because they can no longer pay the market rate. Some landlords take nieces, nephews, or grandkids to the young person's favorite spot in the world as a graduation present. These landlords are fair to their tenants. The international dream trips are possible, in part, because residents pay fair market rents.

How Your Landlording Can Affect Your Legacy

Your legacy choices should guide all your landlording decisions. Good landlords provide clean, safe, and functional housing for their tenants and also increase the value of the property. Scores of our clients live lives worth imitating, and hundreds have created wealth. There are probably as many ways to build legacy through apartment investing as there are investors, but two basic ways dominate.

Some investors' legacy involves how their wealth will be used. These fair and compassionate landlords use their wealth to benefit the world. Their wealth educates their children and helps their relatives. The excess goes to the causes they care about and the church or synagogue they attend.

Other rental owners care more about using their position as landlords, the face-to-face capitalism, to benefit others. These folks are content. They need more money like they need a second nose. How many Mercedes vehicles can you drive at once? How many steaks can you eat? Rather than try to define it, let me share an example.

One of my clients felt called to keep her rental equity near where she grew up, even though the resident profile had changed dramatically. For more than a decade she felt a duty or calling to rent to poor people, and she wanted less affluent people to see how more affluent people worked.

Instead of selling her rentals in a central area and moving the equity to a suburban setting, she kept her equity where most of the residents were minorities. She had enough character, smarts, and relationships that she could have solicited investment from friends and family to buy more or bigger buildings. Instead, for a season, her day-to-day involvement with the residents was more important than creating a rental empire. She interacted with all her tenants and knew all the children by name. She helped several of them through tough times. Her compassion was never a way to buy friends. Being the caring landlady was more important to her than doubling her cash flow or her wealth.

Investing in apartments is one way to build wealth. If you are a good landlord, part of your legacy will be to have people remember you as good and fair. But, for people like my friend, rental ownership offers some unique opportunities to build legacy. I saw this most powerfully because of the life of a person who did not own any apartments.

Tracy worked for one of the best management companies in town. I met her when she worked on our seven-unit apartment building in a neighborhood that makes the nightly news and that your next-door neighbors might consider scary.

She dealt with many first-generation Americans and tenants of all kinds, ethnically diverse, spiritually diverse, racially diverse, and linguistically diverse. When she died, she knew a lot of people, and that's part of the reason that 500+ people showed up at her memorial. One to two hundred people is a typical turnout.

It was standing room only, and the main viewing room was full. They had closed-circuit TVs in other rooms so more people could watch the proceedings. All those rooms were full, too, and there were people outside who just wanted to be there even if they couldn't get inside. That's impressive, but the most impressive thing to me was not that her boss, or her husband or kids, said, "We're going to miss her. She was a wonderful gal." I expected that. What I didn't expect were the tenants who came and swelled the crowd beyond the building's capacity. And I certainly didn't expect one of the speakers to be a tenant telling how Tracy had helped her when she hit a rough patch.

Landlording offers you unique opportunities to create a legacy beyond your wealth. As far as I know, it's the only investment that does that. The way you choose to add value to your property will affect both your legacy and your wealth. The next chapter describes how to add value effectively.

Renovation Budgets and Strategies

"Our main business is not to see what lies dimly in the distance,
but to do what lies clearly at hand."
~ THOMAS CARLYLE

THE SAVVIEST INVESTORS ADD VALUE to their properties by renovating them and increasing the cash flow. Budgeting is a key part of the process. Wise investors determine their renovation strategy when they buy a property and add a little to the budget to account for surprises.

Creating Value for Your Property: Power Tool of Investing

Cash flow from the property is the *dimes*. The wealth building *dollars* come from boosting the income stream, mainly by raising rents or sometimes by lowering costs. Some entrepreneurs talk about *monetizing an income stream* or *having a liquidity event*. Those words mean that other investors will pay you a multiple of the income stream when you sell the property.

Suppose it would cost you $10K to improve the property so you can boost the rents $100 a month. Is that a good idea?

Raising rents $100 a month, $1,200 annually, boosts cash flow. Some owners think this is a terrible idea because it will take more than 8 years to recoup their cash. The bigger truth is that you can sell the income stream for multiples of its value. In many communities, you can sell that income stream for 10 to 15 times the rent. So, if the zip code sells for 12.5 times the income, then the $100 month, or $1,200 a year, just made the property worth $15,000 more: $1,200 annually * 12.5 GRM = $15,000. Fifteen thousand dollars is 50% more than $10,000. That's a 50% return and can be obtained within a year. That growth spurt is terrific for your wealth. Wealth is grown by repeating or extending the growth spurt. In an IPO market, they talk about monetizing the income stream. In effect, that's happening here. The investor who has created more value is selling the income stream. People buy tech stocks not for cash flow but in hopes of selling for higher price. A stock investor can't affect the firm, but a rental owner can change many things about net income.

Creating wealth is when you pay $2 and create $3 of value. Plus, you are also receiving a fine return; a $1,200 cash flow increase from your $10,000 investment is 12% annually. That is dramatically better than stock dividends or bond yields.

There are two ways to measure value of income stream: gross rents and net income. The market pays a multiple of the income, whether it is shown by net or gross income. There is a difference between the multiple of net and gross, and that difference does not matter at this stage. Create more income, and you'll be very glad of it.

You must decide how much to invest to increase the value of your property. For most owners, the basic constraint is the amount of money available for renovation. You set that amount when you determine how much of your Total Cash In you will use for the Down Payment and how much will be in your Rehab Budget. Different renovation strategies require different budgets.

Successful businesses thrive because customers recognize they are receiving good value for their money. Remember that the renter is your customer. Their cash is just as green as yours.

Your financial success depends on your ability to draw and retain residents who will pay good prices to live in your apartments. Great rental owners determine what renters will pay for; then they provide those benefits at the lowest cost. It's a business, like the tech business, restaurant, or clothing store. With face-to-face capitalism, you don't have to pay thousands of dollars for market research. Simply talk to your residents and potential residents. Ask them which is better. Remember the eyeglasses? Which is better, lens A or B? Repeat. Help your residents obtain what they value in a way that benefits you and them.

Renovation Strategies

Essentially, there are three levels of enhancing property values:

- Slightly more than correcting deferred maintenance
- Substantial upgrade
- Repositioning the asset

Slightly more than correcting deferred maintenance

Most likely the building you bought is a little bit tired. The last owner probably deferred some maintenance, and you can limit your renovation to little more than fixing the place up. Here's an example of a building with ten apartments.

Start with the simplest upgrade. You may budget an average of $2,500 per unit ($25,000 overall) to make some modest improvements. About 40% of your budget, or $10,000, can add street appeal. You'll spend that money on some, but not all, of the following: fresh paint with two accent colors, refurbished landscaping, slurry sealing and restriping of the parking lot, having a new or repainted building sign, installing vinyl windows on the street side of the property, power washing, or wrought-iron fencing. You won't be able to do all of that, but whatever you do will make the building look better to prospective residents and current renters. People prefer and will pay more for better-looking property.

San Diego's great weather means our rentals don't have interior hallways. Laundry rooms may be the only common area, so the renovation costs are trivial. If your climate mandates interior hallways and more common area, then your figure will be higher.

Generally, you want the outside to *Pop!* first, to get prospects' attention. Then the interior can convince them that your building should be their next home.

If you spend $10,000 on the exterior, you'll have $15,000 left to spend inside the building over the next year. You'll have to spend some extra money to make modest upgrades beyond the routine "turn" costs of apartments when the current tenants leave. Typical turn costs in San Diego are $1,500 per apartment for a new appliance or ceiling fan if needed, fresh paint, window treatments, carpet cleaning, or maybe replacement and/or repair of faucets, fixtures, countertops, cabinetry, vanity, interior doors, etc. That expenditure returns the apartment to the condition it was when the previous tenant moved in.

Suppose in your market that 40% of the renters move every year. In this prototype building, that could mean you might have four vacancies in the next year. You must spend $1,500 each to make them ready for the new tenant. That money comes out of your operating expenses, but when you have a turn, you also have an opportunity to upgrade the apartment.

Your $15,000 first-year rehab budget gives you an additional $3,750 ($15,000 ÷ 4 vacancies) to enhance each vacancy. When you add that to the $1,500 normal expense, you have more than $5,000 per unit to add value. You could upgrade with some, but not all, of these items: stainless steel appliances, nicer ceiling fan, an accent wall of the color selected by your new resident, all new faucets, fixtures, drawer pulls, all in the same style, maybe brushed nickel, more tile on the floor, or better carpet with a thicker pad, refacing kitchen cabinetry, or a modest bathroom enhancement. You won't be able to do it all, but you can do a lot to upgrade the unit and add value to the property.

California has statewide rent control. In most situations the maximum rent increase is 5% plus consumer price index. State law limits conventional rent increases to 10% annually. If substantial improvements are made then the rents can be raised to the market rate. Law defined substantial renovation as:

- planning on obtaining building permit,

- expecting work will take more than 30 days to complete,

- more work than can be done while the resident is on-site, and

- improving electrical or plumbing systems.

In the past rental owners may have improved cabinetry, countertops, faucets, fixtures, flooring, window treatments, and windows and been able to raise rents significantly. The new law changed what is allowed. My guess as I write this in 2020 is that the number of renovations will drop by more than half in comparison to what we standard in 2016 through 2019.

Because California is a litigious state, the Supreme Court may ultimately be involved in adjudicating these provisions.

Substantial upgrade

To earn a larger increase, you would improve the property further. Suppose you tripled the budget for upgrades to $75,000. Assume a third, $25,000, will be used for exterior work. That amount of renovation can move an asset from slightly tired to among the best on the block.

That leaves $50,000 for interior renovations. You can explain to the tenants that you are planning to improve the property over the next year and that rents will be adjusted as the work is completed. Residents with tight budgets may begin looking for a new home so you will plan on more turns than usual. The plan is to renovate six units, spending the usual $1,500 on each plus $8,125 per unit for upgrades, or almost $10,000 per renovated unit.

Your bigger budget means more and better upgrades, which support even higher rents. In San Diego, a year after purchase, total income could be 7–10% higher. But, as they say on the infomercials, "But wait—there's more!"

Repositioning the asset

Some neighborhoods and some markets offer you an even more dramatic option. A few wise investors will budget $30,000 to $50,000 per unit to reposition the asset. This level of upgrading is not quite to condo standards, but it can move the asset forward a generation or more.

One-inch square tile and lime green and peach were popular in the 1930s. Knotty pine cabinets were chic in previous generations. Shag carpet, avocado green appliances, and burnt orange came and went.

Model homes and architectural magazines reveal today's trends. Home improvement channels erupt with suggestions. Energy efficiency and sustainable landscaping appeal more to this generation of renters. Landlords benefit from lower bills, and residents are glad to be ecologically sensitive. Colors, flooring, and window treatment are each affected by style. IKEA costs less than Ethan Allen; simply choose affordable ways to update the property.

If you choose this option, you may replace 80% or more of the building's tenants in the first year. Upgrades may include new exterior paint with two trim colors, all double-pane vinyl windows, roof, new kitchen cabinetry and quartz or granite countertops, double sinks in kitchen and bath, bathroom vanity, solid surface flooring, baseboards, and maybe crown molding, upgraded lighting, and six-panel doors.

Sometimes there's a creative way to add value. One of my business partners noticed that in the two-bedroom, one-and-a–half-bath units of a building, there was a large closet on the other side of the wall. A licensed plumber and our handyman rearranged sheetrock and plumbing to create a shower in the expanded bathroom. The shower brought $35 higher rent and was a cost-effective improvement. It cost $4,000 to rearrange the wall and include the shower by taking space from the closet; the extra income added almost $6,000 of value.

Each market is different. In some places, astute owners are raising rents 30–70% with this plan. In San Diego, fewer than 10% of investors are employing this strategy. If your market is supply constrained and millennials or other higher-income potential tenants might be drawn into a neighborhood near downtown, this strategy can be investment on steroids.

Business people who add value do well. To add value means to create a profit. The rental owner can sell the income stream. That is the most important power tool of real estate investment. Manufacturers, merchants, and menu creators all consider the perceived value for the consumer and the cost to the producer. If you get into this game, play it well.

Your renovation strategy will determine how much you intend to spend for renovation and how much value you add to your property. It would be great if we could budget perfectly, so we knew exactly how much we were going to spend and when. Alas, apartment investing and life in general are not like that, but there is one thing you can be sure of.

Budgeting for Surprises: 2% Solution

There will be surprises. You never know exactly what they will be—that's why they are called surprises—but you can expect some in your career. Some of them will be good, and you'll consider yourself brilliant or fortunate.

There will also be surprises you don't like. The inspector may be the best in your metro, but no inspector is perfect. He or she can't see inside walls or completely diagnose every detail.

Prudent buyers budget 2% of the purchase price for the unpleasant surprises. Maybe the plumbing leaks or the roof has problems in the first

2 years. Perhaps the sewer has an unexpected backup or a water problem reveals mold, or a window or tub fails. With used cars and with used buildings, there will be surprises.

This 2% budget for surprises is in addition to the rehab budget. Many lenders want income property buyers to have 3–6 months of mortgage payments in reserve. This contingency budget can be part of that extra liquidity the lender wants to see. That idea bears repeating. What you think of as your *Oops!* budget is what your lender may want to see as part of the additional liquidity. Some lenders may wish for 10% of the loan amount, but that does not mean you need to use that lender.

Many assets have surprises, so set aside money for them. When you discover those glitches, relax, because your reserve provides a cushion, the extra liquidity can resolve most of those problems, and you will be in better condition. If you want the people around you to be prudent, then you want to live the values you want them to adopt. You'll be living a life worth imitating.

Hey, you might be lucky; perhaps you are in the fortunate third who don't have any unpleasant surprises. If so, rejoice! If not, just understand it is part of the process of building wealth. It is better to have the cushion and not need it than to need the cushion and not have it.

This book is about building *legacy* wealth. Be remembered as prudent, not foolish. At the memorial for San Diego's most active apartment builder, one of his sons reported that on vacations Dad carried three spare bulbs for the movie projector. When the family was watching home movies in the national park and two bulbs failed, Dad still had the third bulb, so his family could remember their shared history. Live the stories you want to tell and to have told about you.

Adding value to your property is important, but the idea of the wealth escalator is that you will add value, so you can sell at a profit and then purchase another property. The next chapter describes the selling process, from deciding when to sell, through marketing the property, and then negotiating to close.

Successful Selling

"Be quick, but don't hurry."
~ JOHN WOODEN

"You can't always get what you want. But if you try sometimes
you just might find you get what you need."
~ MICK JAGGER

IT'S ABOUT TWO THOUSAND MILES from San Diego, where I live,
to Atlanta. I can drive that at the speed limit in about 30 hours. I could
make the trip at 20 miles per hour, but then it would take more than
100 hours. No driver I know who wants to get to Atlanta would choose
the slower option, but I frequently witness investors who do something
similar. They hold property too long and thus slow down their journey
to legacy wealth.

To build legacy wealth quickly and prudently, you have to pick up the
pace. Buy a property, fix it up, raise the rents and thus the value, and then

move up. This chapter is about the selling part of moving up and building wealth. You'll learn how savvy investors decide when it's time to sell, thus empowering and reemploying their profit. You'll learn how your broker can help you determine your property's market value and how to set a salable price. Then discover how you can simplify the process. And you'll learn about part of the IRS code that can minimize your taxes. We'll start by considering how you decide when it's time to sell.

How to Decide When It's Time to Sell

You'll notice I said *decide* when it's time to sell, not *know* when it's time to sell. The best investors understand that if they want to sell and move up so they can build wealth, they won't suddenly know; they will decide.

There are many triggers for an investor to sell an apartment building. Let's begin with the financial reasons: dollars and cents and prolonging your capital's growth spurt.

My wisest clients regularly review their holdings to ensure their capital is working, not loafing. Many people have a decision rule, even if they don't call it that. An example is the decision rule that "When I've doubled my equity, I'm going to trade up."

I might nudge clients when their equity is coasting instead of working. Another broker might bring an offer that prompts them to act.

There are also nonfinancial reasons to sell. Sometimes a landlord just gets tired of recurring problems. It's possible that the tenant in Unit Seven just wore you out. You tried to move her out, and in effect she said "You've got to sue to evict me. I'm going to haunt you to your grave." And you decide, "I won't put up with her anymore, and I don't want to spend the $1,500 to evict her." Or, perhaps the plumbing problem that you thought you had fixed came back for the third time. When you've just had it with such issues, it may be time to unload the building you own. Those are valid nonfinancial reasons.

Overcoming Human Nature

In some ways, selling a perfectly good property is an unnatural act. Often people don't want to change things unless there's a problem. Selling your property and purchasing another one creates anxiety. You may worry about whether you will make a profitable move or the worst deal of the century. You think about nasty problems that could be lurking in that next property.

People have been shown to be reluctant to part with anything they have, from a coffee cup to an apartment building. As I noted in the Emotional Intelligence chapter, this endowment effect causes people to overvalue what they own, including their apartment building. That's why the first step is for your broker to give you his or her professional opinion of value.

Broker's Opinion of Value

The market sets the price. The owner decides whether he prefers cash or his property. A professional broker will tell the owner the truth, not what the owner wants to hear.

The broker's opinion of value is your broker's estimate of the property's likely appraised value. California law says that brokers can give opinions, but that the word "appraisal" is reserved for people with that license. So even though I give continuing education talks to the fanciest appraisers, Members of Appraisal Institute, MAIs, my estimate of value is not an appraisal. Each state makes its own laws; many don't license appraisers.

My broker's opinion of value will include a written report containing four items:

- An analysis of the latest comparable sales
- What similar property is for sale

- A rental survey
- A recommended list price range.

Appraisers are the disinterested experts hired by lenders who want to make prudent loans. "Prudent" usually means "conservative." Appraisers often determine a lower value for a property than the seller wants or expects. Lenders base their loans for five or more units on the building's cash flow, and then they build in several cushions to minimize the risk of the loan's failing. You'll find details on the process and the math in Appendix D: Loans: How Lenders Determine How Much They'll Lend.

I prefer to present my broker's opinion of value at a formal listing meeting. The owner can review the data and ask any questions about the numbers and calculations or my conclusions.

A great broker will be smart enough to discern the truth, and wise and brave enough to tactfully tell you the truth. Sellers wish their buildings were worth top dollar. Those wishes may be fantasies. And then there's that pesky endowment effect, the human tendency to overvalue the things we own. So I often explain to potential sellers:

> You love your building, but other millionaires who might buy it don't care about many of the things you care about. They just wonder if it is the best way to build their wealth and collect more cash flow.

Regardless of your wishes or fantasies, *the market sets the value*. Perhaps your goal is financial comfort instead of maximizing wealth; you may keep an adequate building and not use your skill to repeat the value-building process. Have you ever seen an indoor plant that was root-bound? Your equity can get trapped in a container, too. If your goal is wealth building, freeing your equity from a smaller asset and promoting it to a bigger asset will produce a better result. Don't keep the general doing the private's work.

If you want to build wealth, the biggest mistake is to dawdle in a currently good position when a better result is achievable. Since you have boosted property value once, you can probably repeat that feat with a larger asset.

The wise investor adopts the idea that reality is your friend. Your great broker has spent years or decades honing his or her craft. Ask questions to help you understand your broker's facts and reasoning. Your broker will help you understand reality so that you can act on it, beginning with setting a sensible price for your building.

Pricing to Sell

Setting an appropriate listing price is both art and science. The listing price should be high enough to provide some negotiating room and to learn what the market will pay. The listing price should be low enough to arouse several buyers' interest. Smart listing brokers suggest a price that will promptly obtain realistic offers. Our team often sets the initial listing price about 10% above what we think the appraisal value will be. Then the market takes over.

In a rising market a fabulous broker helps the client buy. Alternately, in a falling market, a terrific broker gets the assets sold. Candidly, most brokers seem to react slowly to market turns. The experts increase the client's chance of moving in the right direction during transitions and times of chaos.

Excellent brokers shift from explaining truth in the listing presentation to focusing on advocating for seller's property. Like a masterful attorney, they know the truth and then they frame their case to help their client win.

Our team sells the future potential income of your property to a rich stranger who will probably never do business with you again. That rich stranger is as close as you will ever be to the rational actor that the economists believe in. Smart investors will compare your opportunity to several others. They'll buy your property *if, and only if,* they're convinced it's their best option. In other words, it will be just like when you bought the property, except this time you're the seller.

The buyer's broker usually does the initial screening. That broker must believe your property is reasonably priced. Brokers don't waste time on unrealistic listings because they are paid for results, not for educating somebody else's client. So the greedy fool who lists a property far above the market will receive few, if any, offers.

A buyer's broker who thinks your property is fairly priced will notify the buyer. Your broker's reputation plays an important role here. If other brokers know that your broker's listings usually sell, they're more likely to decide that your listing is realistic and tell their client about it. For example, because my closing ratio is far higher than the average in San Diego, brokers are more likely to forward my listing to their clients.

When you receive serious offers, you know the property has a chance of selling. In most years, in San Diego County, if you haven't gotten an offer in the most recent 60 days, then your property is probably overpriced. When we enter a recession, our pricing is softer. For example, if prices are or might soon be falling, we suggest a list price based on what the asset would have appraised for last month. Values might be down 5 or 10% within 6 to 12 months, so our team wants our clients out of the market as soon as possible. Better for the client to have cash rather than an asset whose value is melting.

Pricing is only part of what makes a successful sale. If you want the best results, both you and your broker have things to do. Let's begin by reviewing the marketing process.

Minimizing Obstacles to a Successful Sale

In the late 1950s, comedy duo Bob Elliott and Ray Goulding starred in a famous series of ads for Piels beer, a New York brand. The ads were wildly popular, and Piels' sales increased—but not for long. People liked the ads, tried the beer, and discovered it wasn't very good. The lesson is that good marketing should paint a realistic picture of your property, but good marketing can't offset bad value. You can improve the way your property appears to buyers. These steps are fairly easy, and similar to what you would do to sell a house.

Over time, I've become more strategic in preparing the marketing message. We like to see the inside of a few units before receiving the first offer. We prefer to see the best and worst unit, so we can identify or avoid potential problems and set reasonable expectations for buyers and their brokers. Negative surprises are powerful psychological events. Potential buyers might interpret a negative surprise as evidence that you're untrustworthy and move on to another property.

Sprucing up Your Property's Exterior

A potential buyer will drive by first. They know they're buying a used apartment building, but it's wise to maximize your property's street appeal, given the location. Consider these simple things you can do to the exterior of the building:

- Powerwash the building and driveways
- Paint the trim
- Buff the landscaping
- Routinely pick up litter

If there's grass, make sure it's green, mown, and edged. Shrubs and trees should be neatly trimmed. Remove any dead plants, even if you don't replace them. Consider planting some colorful flowers. Even if they're dead by the time escrow opens, they will have done their job.

We take photos and order the drone video to show property in the best possible light. The drone video highlights the best features of the property and the area. The buyer can see the interiors without disturbing any residents. The drone video displays unique features, area redevelopment, nearby amenities, and other things we want to feature. Roofs are one of the biggest potential costs of a used building. The drone allows people to preview the roof. The drone video diminishes the chance that a rogue "wannabe" buyer will knock on a tenant's door, announce that the building is for sale, and ask to see the inside. That rude behavior is uncommon, but unfortunately not all buyers are courteous or well advised.

Sprucing up the interiors

Send your handyman through all the units. Fix any small problems such as leaky faucets. Ask residents if the appliances, heaters, and air conditioners work. If there are ceiling stains from a previous roof or toilet leak that has been fixed, use KILZ® to repaint the ceiling. Keep the laundry room tidy. Solving minor problems before the inspection minimizes concessions after the inspection.

Every situation is different. These fixes are inexpensive, but sometimes novel measures are appropriate. One of our listings had unusually bad housekeepers. The seller hired a cleaning service to go in the day before the physical inspection to put away some clutter, vacuum carpets, and clean bathrooms. It worked; we closed.

Dealing with building challenges

No property is perfect. If there are significant problems such as a cracked slab, environmental contamination, a flat roof more than 8 years old, or other costly items, notify your broker as soon as possible. Assume that all secrets will be revealed. It is best to adjust expectations first and not risk having to repair both the building and your relationship with the buyer.

Dealing with an on-site manager

This issue can be sensitive. Every choice has risks. If you have an on-site manager or contact person at your property, consider how they will learn that the property is on the market. If you were the on-site manager, how would you want to be treated? In most cases, it is probably best that they are aware of your plans. Your choices may affect them substantially. The new owner may or may not retain the existing on-site manager. State laws vary on what number of units can be operated without an on-site manager. California law requires an on-site manager for 16 or more units.

An up-front discussion will generally help facilitate the manager's cooperation, and it gives you an opportunity to clarify what they should and should not do if someone comes looking. For instance, if a possible buyer is on the property and asks to see a vacant unit without an appointment, will you want the manager to comply? This type of issue should be clarified at the beginning of a listing.

Some owners have offered the on-site manager a bonus ranging from $100 to a month's compensation if the property sells during the listing period. It is cheap insurance, and it generates good will.

When a manager learns that a property is on the market, the manager might leave. Remind the manager that not all listings sell, and that the new owner will need a good manager.

However, if someone other than you tells them that you are selling, the manager may be hurt and less likely to cooperate further.

Notifying residents

Our experience has shown that a "For Sale" sign in front of property brings in a few more buyer inquiries and rarely causes tenants to leave. However, some owners fear having a sign out front.

In that case, some residents may ask you or the resident manager if the building is for sale. Think about your response before the question comes up. When there is no "For Sale" sign, usually the first time most residents will know the property is for sale is after you have an accepted offer, when the buyer is inspecting the individual units.

There is an unlikely possibility that an unsophisticated buyer will approach the residents. Such discussions are rare and beyond your control.

The worst that could occur is that the residents ask you if the building is for sale, before you tell them it is in escrow.

Title

Some investors hold property alone and have never had any unusual activity affecting title. Others have partners, divorce, death, taxes, liens, judgments, or other title complications. If you know anything that might slow the process of obtaining clear title, let your broker know. These issues are almost always resolvable, but some take extra time.

Representing your property's condition

Most smart buyers will ask the seller to warrant that as of the close of escrow, the roof has no known leaks, that the appliances, including heaters, air conditioners, and heat pumps, work and that there are no major problems with the electrical or plumbing systems.

If there are not any problems, we'll negotiate one way. If there are big problems, we'll negotiate differently. The most important thing is that you and your broker know the actual condition of your building. Otherwise, things become unnecessarily complicated.

One of my peers represented a seller who told the broker and the buyer that everything worked and that there were no problems. The buyer asked for warranties and the seller agreed. Unbeknown to the seller, none of the heaters worked. During the inspection, this truth was discovered. The seller bought all new heaters a week before the close of escrow. If the seller had known the truth earlier, a good broker could have marketed the property as needing tender loving care and might have saved the seller some cash.

More than 90% of our listings receive an offer high enough that the buyer and seller eventually agree on a price. When the buyer and the seller have agreed upon basic price and terms, the due-diligence process begins. See Appendix C for details. Know that the buyer will inspect the entire property.

If we know what the inspector will find before the inspection, there is less chance of losing the deal. The truth is the truth, whether you and your broker know it or not. The sooner you and the buyer know the truth, the better. Learning the truth early in the process equips your broker to market your property more effectively.

How We Market Properties

After setting a reasonable list price, a competent broker will systematically and aggressively promote the opportunity to brokers and buyers. Here is how our team has achieved superior closing success rates over the last generation.

We aim to gather the most important property details before listing it. We'll learn special features, amenities, and other reasons that could cause it to be a superior opportunity. Recent capital expenditures like roof replacements and other upgrades can mean lower costs or higher potential rents for the next buyer. We package the asset's potential in ways to generate maximum appeal. Your broker will ask you questions. Tell him or her why you picked the property, why residents choose it, what else might be done to boost rents or lower expenses, and anything else that could make your building better than the competition's.

Within days of receiving the signed listing contract, we post information in the San Diego County Investment Multiple Listing Service. Within a week, we advertise in Loopnet.com, our company website, my personal site (SanDiegoApartmentBroker.com), and through them to scores of other sites. Buyers of big-ticket items, including rentals, conduct their preliminary research on the web. We make it easy for Internet users to know about the property.

We also mail to the owners of the county's 10,500 largest apartment buildings. We email marketing materials to thousands of investors and the income brokers who close more than a third of the county's apartment business. We contact potential buyers and their brokers to let them know about the listing.

Unlike many of our competitors, we promptly and actively solicit the involvement of other competent investment brokers. We present the opportunity at routine marketing meetings with other hyperactive peers and competitors.

Personal meetings with investors are the point of all the letters, calls, and ads. We can discreetly tour the property with investors, and request that other brokers do the same.

Some sellers prefer frequent contact, while others don't want to be bothered until they need to act. We tailor our feedback cycle and methods to what the client prefers: emails, calls, documents, reports.

No one can guarantee buyer behavior, but our clients know that our marketing works. Your broker's system will be different, but you need an agent whose success or closing rate is well above average. Some brokers close little and list much. They may be either new to the business or suffer "big hat and few cattle," or "all talk, no action" syndrome.

Next let's focus on how you can increase your odds of success.

When You Have an Offer

In most successful transactions, there are several negotiations after you and your broker select the list price. Your most important negotiation with the buyer will be at the beginning regarding price and terms. After the inspections, however, many sophisticated buyers ask for concessions.

That's when you and the buyer will decide if you want a good excuse or a good result. It's easy to get hooked emotionally or become unnerved by an aggressive negotiator on the other side of the table. The best negotiation strategy suggests focusing on the interests, not personalities or position. Know your next best alternative. Three seller's/owner's possibilities are to wait for another buyer, renovate the property and hold it, or refinance.

Don't be distracted by the buyer's actions or attitude. Remember Stephen R. Covey's advice: "Begin with the end in mind."

If the buyer or agent is rude, but you walk away with more money than your next best opportunity, it probably makes sense to close the transaction. Some clients wasted from $5K to $150K because they were going to "teach them a lesson in good faith bargaining." It is not your job to teach the other side lessons they should have learned in kindergarten. Your job and your broker's job is to get your property sold.

There might be another negotiation if the lender won't grant the desired loan. Perhaps the appraiser values the asset below the contract price, or the underwriter doubts the property's ability to service the loan. A great broker will warn you if the contract price may exceed likely appraisal value. If the buyer can't get the loan, he or she may cancel the deal, or make a larger down payment, or ask you to carry a second trust deed on another property, or ask you to reduce the price.

Don't worry about what you cannot control. Always consider what your next best alternative is, and keep your cool as you move toward the close.

Physical inspection

In the past, investors would sometimes buy a property based on seeing the building's exterior and a few of the units. Not anymore.

Know that prudent buyers will expect to see *all* units, *all* the garages, and *all* the storage areas. They will probably have an inspector, contractor, or handyman accompany them. Expect them to look at the roof, the foundation, and everything in between.

In ideal circumstances, the buyer comes once and only once to see the inside. The property manager or resident manager lets them into all the units. Generally, sellers prefer that buyers not visit inside again. A second inspection increases the risk that the buyer will ask for concessions because they may notice more things about the used property.

Escrow and closing

Escrow ensures that all the money is credited to the correct parties when title is transferred. In San Diego, escrow prorates rents and taxes based upon the number of days each party owns the property. Resident deposits will be credited to the new owner.

In San Diego, sellers are better off closing after all the rents have been collected. Often escrow credits the buyer for rents, regardless of whether the seller has collected them. If the seller doesn't collect all the rent before the close, the task is harder because the former landlord has no leverage. I recommend that the seller work with slow-paying tenants, even offering them a discount for prompt payment in the seller's final month of ownership.

Finally, notify utilities, trash, and laundry firms of the day escrow will close. Have money removed from the laundry machines the last day you own the building.

Make arrangements with your broker, your property management firm, or resident manager for transferring keys, leases, rental applications, and warranties, which the new owner will need. Also, buyers often appreciate sellers who share their list of service providers.

Remember, the last month's rents are prorated. Some bills will come in after the close of escrow. Don't spend all the cash before the bills are paid. If you are doing a tax-deferred exchange, which we'll discuss in detail in the next chapter, it may be best to pay most bills before the close of escrow.

Just in case there is some last obstacle or annoyance (unforeseen transaction expense, buyer seeks an extra half-percent concession, or whatever), remember your long-term goal. Forgive an analogy, if you have a great summer vacation in Yosemite, you might get a mosquito bite. Don't sweat the small stuff.

In both money-changing and in language, something is lost in translation. However, the benefit of communication is worth the minor imprecision; call it *the translation friction*. Your equity has value. To trade up you need cash, which is universally accepted. Remember, real estate equity has immense value, but it is not as liquid as cash. An owner may conclude a property is worth a million dollars, but within a 180-day period he may sell for $990K because he needs the cash to buy a bigger asset with more potential.

I recall the story of a rich man who was extremely thirsty on the African safari. He didn't have the national currency to pay for the water he wanted. The local money changer wanted a huge spread to convert currencies. The rich man needed the water, so he gave the equivalent of $5 and bought the cool water he needed. Over the course of the trip, the difference was miniscule. He would have been a fool to pass out from dehydration in the Land Rover.

He may have told the story of the greedy money changer many times. Some people relish telling victim stories. Do you want that to be part of your heritage, or would you rather be known as a person who enjoyed creation and focused on the lovely, true, and helpful things? Keep the end in mind. Live and tell the stories you want to be remembered for.

One more important detail related to selling: Don't forfeit a third of your capital gain before the next acquisition. One of the best wealth-building strategies is to keep your full equity working for you. The IRS tax code has a special real-estate benefit known as the *1031 exchange*. That's the subject of the next chapter.

1031 Exchange

"You must pay taxes. But there's no law that says
you gotta leave a tip."
~ Morgan Stanley advertisement

You and your broker aren't the only ones who want you to sell your building. The IRS and your local state tax authority want some of your profit. That's because if you sell and receive cash, you might pay as much as a third of your profits to the government . . . far sooner than you need to.

Each year you own income property, you can deduct the supposed decreased value of the building, called depreciation. When you sell the building for a profit, the tax authority will recognize that the value went up, not down. They will "recapture" that depreciation. In other words, they will treat all earlier depreciation as ordinary income, because you previously deducted the deprecation against ordinary income.

Together the Internal Revenue Service and your state impose four different taxes. The IRS will recapture all depreciation you have taken and you owe taxes at ordinary-income-tax rates. This "extra income" above and beyond your regular income may push you into a higher tax bracket. Then there are federal capital gains taxes on the difference between what you paid for the property and what you sold it for. The Affordable Care Act, also known as "Obamacare," taxes "unearned income." That's just the federal government. Your state tax authority also expects tax based on your profit. Expect 25–40% of your profit to go for taxes if you receive that profit in cash and/or a note.

You have to pay these taxes, but you don't have to pay them early. You can legally minimize your tax bill. Judge Learned Hand is the lower court judge most quoted by legal scholars and by the Supreme Court. In 1934, he heard the case of *Helvering* (the IRS Commissioner) *v. Gregory* and wrote:

> Any one may so arrange his affairs that his taxes shall be as low as possible; he is not bound to choose that pattern which will best pay the Treasury; there is not even a patriotic duty to increase one's taxes.

The IRS code gives real estate investors a unique break not offered to investors in stock or bonds. Internal Revenue Code, section 1031, allows a taxpayer to defer taxes on capital gains. Deferring taxes is different from avoiding taxes. Deferring means that tax is owed, but not yet due. Tax-deferred exchange, also known as "1031 exchange" or simply "1031," is available to any real estate investor.

Deferring your taxes is like receiving an interest-free loan, equal to the taxes you owe, from the government. All your equity continues working for you, which also helps your community and the national economy. There are no good-citizen points for surrendering a third of your profit early. Here's how the 1031 exchange works.

Instead of paying taxes early, all your wealth can work for you until you die. Tax laws change. Estate tax or death tax has come and gone several times. As of this book's initial publication date, estate taxes are in place, and current tax law values the inheritance based on its market value at date of death, rather than its cost. Most real estate is worth more at owner's death than when it was purchased. The increased value is called "stepped up" basis. So, the heirs inherit at its then-current value, not the purchase price. In effect, the family never has to pay capital gains or depreciation recapture: They skip that tax; they disinherit the IRS. Your CPA or investment broker will know whether the stepped basis rule is still in place when you sell.

For example, my mom predeceased my dad. Dad received Mom's half of the property at a value based on the year of Mom's passing. Two years later, Dad met his Maker. My wife and I received a huge legacy (compassion, courage, courtesy, forgiveness, grit, integrity, etc.), and the tiny inheritance from my parents. Because the estate was less than $5 million, my wife and I paid no inheritance tax. Mom and Dad left their home and a small commercial investment. The value at Dad's date of death, rather than the cost, was how the taxing authority valued the estate. For IRS purposes, our value and thus our depreciation value were reset at date of death. In effect, my parents disinherited the tax man.

Hundreds of my clients have benefited from these IRS regulations, which are specific and nonnegotiable. Intelligent planning and careful action have deferred capital gains for millions.

Here are the major requirements to obtain tax deferral:

- The purchase/sale document and escrow instructions should show the taxpayer's intent to complete a 1031 exchange.
- An accommodator, like an escrow agent, must be used to hold your proceeds until you close on the acquisition property.
- Within 45 days of the closing of the sale property, the taxpayer must identify the potential acquisition property.
- Within 180 days (which is different from six months), the taxpayer must complete the acquisition of the new property.

- The acquisition property must be acquired for investment or business use; primary residences or vacation homes don't qualify.

- The taxpayer must acquire a new property of equal or greater value than the disposed property.

- The new debt must be equal to or greater than the disposition debt.

Other rules include limitations on buying from or selling to related parties, like immediate family; details about how many properties can be identified; prohibitions against the taxpayer's having access to the proceeds while those proceeds are in the accommodator (think escrow) account; and which people the IRS will recognize as an accommodator.

Superb investment brokers, many CPAs who specialize in real estate investment accounting, and commercial escrow agents at the national title companies can guide you through the appropriate procedures. Some intricate details might call for a tax attorney. A great investment broker or commercial escrow agent with 1031 experience can guide most investors and don't charge a high hourly fee. A true professional will tell you when a more specialized expert is needed.

You must follow the rules to obtain the immense benefits. That takes work, but it's work that will pay you a top hourly rate.

Regulations

Complying with the IRS regulations makes a 1031 exchange like receiving an interest-free loan equal to the tax you owe. You don't pay taxes yet and there is no interest cost to you.

The IRS wants to know your motivation. Document your intent to use 1031 exchange in both sales and purchase contracts. The property you sell is called the disposed, sold, or downleg property. The property you buy is called your acquisition, upleg, or purchased property. From now on, *downleg* means sold property and *upleg* means purchased property. In an audit, you need to show your intent to exchange in the sales contract for both the downleg and the upleg.

However, if it's two days before the close of escrow and you say, "I don't want to pay a third of my profit to taxes. Let me do a tax-deferred exchange," an IRS audit may mean that you'll pay taxes because your intent was not obvious from the beginning.

Budget Implications

If you plan to buy another property with the "right things wrong with it" and fix it up, think about your rehab budget for your upleg property and your 1031 exchange. You'll need some extra renovation cash for your 1031 property. Perhaps you could come up with the renovation money from your savings or income. If so, there are no tax implications, and all the proceeds from your 1031 sale can be the down payment for your next property. Alternatively, you can use some of the sales proceeds to renovate your next property, but then you will have to pay some taxes on the sales proceeds you used. Both tactics work.

For example, if you need $50K of the proceeds from your sale for renovation, then you could receive $75K of sale proceeds to complete the renovations and pay your expected tax bill on the $75K proceeds not used for down payment, called "boot." You use $50K immediately on the renovations and pay the $25K in taxes next April 15.

Your broker or expert CPA can guide you to your best option. Often, a better solution would be to borrow $50K on line of credit against your home or other asset. That would be cheaper than giving up $25K a generation too early. We tell our clients about other options.

Time Extension

The IRS tax code specifies various timeline and transaction markers. The defining event that starts the schedule is close of escrow.

Remember the property you sell is called the downleg. By the 45th day after you close on the downleg, you must identify in writing to your accommodator what you're going to buy. Three different rules in the code govern this, but most investors choose the rule that says they will specify no more than three properties. Between the close of escrow and your 45th day, you can look at many properties. But on your 45th day, you must notify your accommodator in writing that you intend to buy one, two, or three specific properties. Fax, email, or certified delivery all provide time stamps, which can be vital in case of an audit.

Then you must close on a property within 180 days from the date of escrow. If the 180th day occurs on a weekend or holiday, you must close before that day. Talk with your broker, CPA, or accommodator to ensure you're clear about timing. There are a couple of other details.

To give you extra time to identify your acquisition property, you can extend your sale escrow. That detail is best negotiated at time of sale with the buyer. Essentially your broker puts it to the buyer this way:

> Seller must have the right to extend the escrow once for 30 days, or maybe twice for 30 days. That's nonnegotiable. If you buy this property, seller gets this option. If you can't do it, seller will select another buyer.

Here's an example. Suppose that you own the Paradise Apartments, and I'm your broker. We market them, negotiate with several buyers, and enter escrow with your best option. Usually, the buyer needs 6–8 weeks to inspect the property and obtain a loan.

After buyer has waived the physical inspection contingency (usually 17 days in California), you, the seller, should begin looking in earnest for the upleg property. A week before the close of escrow, if you've got an acceptable property, then you say "Wahoo, let's go ahead and close." Alternatively, we may decide to exercise your extension option.

In that case, we can extend the escrow by a month or two. If you don't extend, the reality is you probably have about 90 days to make your choice. You'll have about 6 weeks while the buyer is obtaining financing, and then

45 days after the close of escrow. But when we exercise a 30-day extension or two, you can get a fourth or a fifth month to identify your upleg property.

We've reached the end of The Wealth Escalator, where you learned the basics of buying, operating, and selling apartments to build your legacy wealth. Turn the page for a recap of key points.

Wealth Escalator Summary

BEFORE YOU MOVE ON to the Your Investment Life Trajectory section, let's review these important points about The Wealth Escalator. You and your broker will repeat this cycle as you build your legacy wealth. For more details about any of these highlights, see the chapter indicated in parentheses.

Intelligent apartment investing demands hard work from you and your broker, but done correctly it can produce legacy wealth. (A Practical Way to Prioritize Opportunities)

My process blends systematic, low-tech analysis with your personal emotional and economic goals and available options so you can identify and capture the best opportunity for you. (A Practical Way to Prioritize Opportunities)

The multiple-offers strategy gives you two benefits: increased closing speed and better choice of properties. The Offer Dashboard simplifies tracking your options as you write multiple offers. (Successful Buying)

Writing backup offers increases your odds of acquiring your best available property. (Successful Buying)

A bias for action and a propensity to pounce when you identify an excellent opportunity enables you to capture best opportunity. Don't let a nimbler competitor snatch your best option. (Successful Buying)

Not everyone should be a landlord. Wise owners respect tenants and improve the value of the property. (Successful Operating)

Landlording offers you many choices about the best way for you to build legacy wealth. Your desired legacy should drive your decisions about who will handle property management and maintenance, setting rents, and adding value to your property. (Successful Operating)

Creating value for your property is the "Power Tool of Investing." (Renovation Budgets and Strategies)

Great rental owners determine what tenants want and will pay for. Then they provide those benefits at the lowest cost. (Renovation Budgets and Strategies)

There are three levels of enhancing property value. You can increase the value just a bit more than correcting deferred maintenance. You can upgrade the property substantially. Some properties present the opportunity to do even more and reposition the asset. (Renovation Budgets and Strategies)

Whatever option you choose, budget for surprises. There will always be surprises. (Renovation Budgets and Strategies)

Successful apartment investors' bias for action also enables you to recognize when it's time to sell and to price the asset so it will attract offers. (Successful Selling)

Successful sales usually result from a realistic price, combined with aggressive marketing and removing common obstacles to a sale. Two or three negotiations usually take place after you and your broker select the list price. After the inspections, many sophisticated buyers ask for concessions. (Successful Selling)

With intelligent planning and careful action, many smart apartment investors use section 1031 of the IRS code to defer taxes while they build their legacy wealth. (See 1031 Exchange)

The Greek philosopher Heraclitus said that you can't step into the same river twice. The river is always flowing and changing, like life. You can use the basic tools and processes of The Wealth Escalator for the rest of your life, but your life and the market will change. The next section shows you how to adapt your legacy wealth building to differing circumstances.

Your Investment Life Trajectory

This section's three chapters consider how your investment goals may change with passing decades.

Prolonging Your Capital's Growth Spurt describes the two ways you extend your capital's ride on the wealth escalator.

No matter how successful you are at apartment investing, you may decide another vehicle or goal is better. The **Moving On** chapter outlines four common answers to an investor's question, "What's next?"

In **Transferring Your Legacy Wealth**, I'll share three common ways millionaires attempt to keep their wealth in their family and why they're rarely successful. Then we'll consider how to transfer your legacy wealth to benefit your family and the causes you support.

Prolonging Your Capital's Growth Spurt

"Discipline is remembering who you are
or who you want to be."
~ TERRY MOORE

DON'T EXPECT TO ACHIEVE YOUR LEGACY WEALTH by buying, fixing up, and selling a single apartment building. To achieve legacy wealth, you must repeat the process in the investment cycle several times. Your challenge will be to keep your capital growing. This chapter tells two ways successful investors extend the growth spurt.

Let's suppose you invested in a property a few years ago. Now your equity has grown, and you want to keep it growing. There are two superior options. You can trade up—sell the building and buy another property; or you can refinance and use the cash as down payment for the next purchase. Either way, you're going to redeploy your equity so it works harder for you. Let's consider the trade-up option first.

Trading Up Is the Core Strategy

Trading up is the core strategy most clients use to build legacy wealth. Investors in rapidly rising markets tend to do better by acquiring more property sooner. In San Diego, far more real estate millionaires created their wealth by trading up than by refinancing and purchasing bigger assets. And trading up offers some other advantages.

Frequently, appraisers value a sale to an unrelated or "arm's length" buyer, above what they can on a refinance. In San Diego County, for example, a building which might appraise for $950K on refinance could easily sell for $1 million to a new purchaser.

An appraiser searches for similar properties near the subject that have closed recently. These sales are called *comparables*, or *comps*. For a refinance that is the best information available. Alternatively, when the subject property is in escrow and an unrelated stranger is offering to buy it, that is another data point. So, the appraiser has more information on a sale and can consider the extra fact that a disinterested third party will pay $1 million or more for the building. That extra truth shows the lender and the regulators that the appraiser is prudent.

Lenders are conservative. Often, they lend a lower percentage on a refinance than on new purchase. A bank may lend 60% of the refinance amount ($950K), a loan amount of $570K to the current owner. But the same bank might lend 65% of the purchase price ($1 million), so they might lend $650K to a new buyer on the same building.

Lenders are also more conservative on "cash-out refinance" than they are on acquisition loan. It is common for half of the equity to be imprisoned in the first building ever after cash-out refinance.

When you trade up, you can access all your capital, not just the portion the lender will advance. Buyers who have more liquid capital can generate more and larger transactions. Looking at more opportunities increases the likelihood of capturing a superior purchase. And, when you combine trading up with a 1031 exchange, you also defer taxes on your gains.

Refinancing

Sometimes investors refinance a property. Here's why.

When you refinance, your transaction costs are lower than trading up; there is no real estate brokerage cost. You only pay for refinance and any prepayment on your current loan. In California, long-term ownership offers property-tax advantages, and refinancing does not cause a reassessment. California reassesses property tax only when an asset sells.

Many millionaires have built legacy wealth. Our team studies our wisest clients and shares the best practices with the rest of our clients. Each client selects their path to building wealth. After decades, some investors diversify or move equity into other asset classes. The next chapter highlights other investment real estate options.

Moving On

> "To every thing there is a season, and a time
> to every purpose under the heaven."
> ~ Ecclesiastes 3:1

Congratulations!

You set out to obtain financial freedom by investing in residential income property. By a combination of brilliance, grit, hard work, luck, skill, and all the rest, you have obtained your financial goals. Well done!

Now what?

Perhaps you may shift from apartment investing. You may tire of tenants, trash, and toilets. Maybe more cash flow, limited management, and security of high-credit tenants will become more important than more appreciation.

Chuck and Jane are in that position. Think of them as Mark and Sharon at a later stage of life. Chuck and Jane became financially independent by investing in apartments, following the principles in this book. Their children are grown and out of college. Chuck and Jane are ready for the next stage of their life.

Time is precious to them. They want to spend it with their children, grandchildren, and friends. They're ready for the trips they've talked about for decades. They don't need more wealth. Now is the time to live out the next third of their lives.

Moving on is what this chapter is about. You'll learn about four common alternatives for apartment investors and the trade-offs of each one. Chuck and Jane can exchange their apartments for a different product type, or they can sell their property and carry the mortgage, or they can simply sell, pay taxes, and live a simpler life. Let's consider the low risk, almost-no-management exchange option first. The most common version is a *single-tenant triple-net asset.*

Invest in a Single-Tenant Triple-Net, "NNN" Property

Chuck and Jane can use a 1031 exchange to move their equity from apartments to a commercial property rented to a national firm with very high credit rating, such as a chain drug store, fast-food chain, or a major bank.

Single-tenant triple-net (NNN) properties are the lowest vacancy-risk investment real estate. Lowest risk is different from risk free. *Single tenant* means that only one business leases the property. *Triple net* means the landlord receives a check net of taxes, net of insurance costs, net of all other property-related costs. I'm ignoring the barber who rents a building, but instead am focusing on investment-grade or bond-rated tenants. Fortune 500 companies may have such good credit that they can sell their unsecured debt to private investors. Bonds are unsecured debt. They are based on the "full faith and credit" of the issuer. Even Fortune 500 companies have some credit risk, but it is dramatically smaller than the ordinary apartment asset.

NNN properties provide investors these benefits:

- Lowest risk because the national commercial tenants have bond-rated credit

- Long-term leases

- Rent increases that almost keep up with inflation
- "Almost no management–almost no worry" income
- A variety of potential tenants and locations
- Simplified estate planning

NNN assets concentrate a large portion of their net worth in a single asset. The risks of vacancy and rapidly increasing expenses are far smaller than for most investment real estate.

For the corporations who lease these properties, location is the key to profitability, so they do extensive analysis of every location. They review traffic patterns, employment and population trends, and extensive demographic data to determine the best location. That thorough analysis happens before the investor ever sees the building.

Lowest risk does not mean risk free. Over the next 50 years the tenant might go bankrupt or not renew the lease. If that happens, a local commercial broker could lease the space to another tenant.

If something changed for one business, the people, income, and traffic that made the location a first choice for one firm will probably appeal to another company. Most investment real estate brokers lease commercial space. Those experts routinely re-lease office, retail, and industrial space. Their signs are in front of many retail, office, and industrial assets—"Available: Bob Broker, Investment Real Estate 888-555-1234."

Most investors purchase NNN more than a two-hour drive away from the investor's home. No matter where you live, most Americans live more than two hours away from you. San Diego County has about 1% of the nation's population. That means 99% of Americans live outside my county; 87% live outside my state. NNN properties are proportional to population, so 99% of the NNN buildings are outside San Diego County, and 87% are outside California.

People may buy property near their favorite grandchild or another preferred destination. "If we're going to buy a CVS drug store, then let's pick one close to Mary." They visit their investment property and write off the trip . . . and just happen to visit someone or someplace close by.

One more thing: People notice that a few chains are closing some stores. That might be scary, but a close analysis reveals that the closed locations are almost entirely in malls. Internet sales are growing faster than sales for brick-and-mortar locations. The chains that rent single-tenant properties are expanding.

The typical NNN lease will go from 10 to 30 years. Many will have a series of 5-year options after the main lease. Over 1,000 companies rent in NNN buildings. Each tenant develops a standard lease for all their stores. The lease is drawn by the tenant's attorney. A prudent investor will have the lease reviewed by a trusted advisor, perhaps a real estate attorney or the income property broker who is familiar with these leases. In most cases, you're buying an asset from another investor, not from the builder of the structure, nor the company that is leasing the property. You cannot change the lease; you can accept it or not.

Typically, the lease payments are flat for about 5 years, and then there is an increase of maybe 10%; then it's flat for another 5 years. So, over 20 years, if the lease goes up 10% four times, the cumulative rent increase will compound to slightly more than 40%. Over the past hundred years, U.S. inflation has averaged near 3% per year. This means that the tenant is gradually getting a slightly better lease on an inflation-adjusted basis. If the owner is age 75 and doesn't expect to live to age 115, the slippage to inflation is true, but irrelevant.

The inflation difference actually increases the likelihood that the tenant will renew. After 10 years, tenants may be renting space 10% cheaper on an inflation-adjusted basis. The longer they stay, the bigger their incentive to remain. As the investor ages, that means less chance of the tenant's moving.

NNN investments provide low-risk cash flow with minimum management responsibilities. They're not the best vehicles to build wealth.

Move Equity to Commercial Property

NNN assets are one common next step for investors who move equity away from apartments, but there are other options. Office, industrial, and retail assets appeal to many investors. Like all of life and investing, there are trade-offs.

Many cities have more $10-million commercial buildings than $10-million apartment properties. Landlords hope that businesses are more economically stable than households. Commercial buildings tend to have less human drama that requires landlord intervention. The leases usually run 3–7 years, with both good and bad features. Some investors perceive commercial property to be easier to manage or to have more bragging rights than apartments. On the other hand, it can take months to fill vacant commercial space, and there is a hefty leasing brokerage cost. Filling a vacant apartment in 1–2 weeks is often easy and does not require a brokerage fee.

Most commercial tenants want the space modified. The landlord allows some figure, say $20 per square foot, to customize the space. If the tenant wants more amenities, then the cost of the extra is amortized over the lease. If the 5,000-square-foot tenant is OK with a $20-per-square-foot allowance, that means the landlord pays the contractor $100K for the work, tenant improvements, or "TIs," to be done before the tenant moves in.

But not every landlord has a spare $100K in the bank. If the tenant will rent 10,000 square feet or wants $40-per-square-foot improvements, then $100K is not enough.

With commercial space, a commercial broker or two are paid a leasing fee, often maybe 5% of the total lease value. For example, assume the lease payment was $10K a month for 5 years, or $600K total consideration. The brokers usually expect half of their $30K fee upon the signing of the lease and the balance when the tenant moves in.

Nationally, commercial properties have higher vacancy rates than multifamily. During recessions, many businesses are hurt or scared, so a vacancy in hard times is usually harder to fill than an apartment. And, as you learned earlier, government regulators have determined that loans on office, industrial, and retail bear twice the risk of apartment loans, so the commercial loan rates and terms for these properties are not as good.

Carry the Mortgage on the Sale of Your Property

Another option involves carrying the mortgage yourself when you sell your asset. An installment sale spreads the tax consequences over time. The down payment is taxed in the year it is received. There are several components to the tax: recapture of depreciation, capital gains tax, the affordable care (Obamacare) "unearned income" tax, and state income tax. In the following years, the seller/lender pays ordinary income tax on the interest received and pays the other taxes on the principal received that year.

Many investors like the installment sale because:

- Sellers know the property and the area
- Sellers are slowly weaned away from their long-held investment
- If the buyer stumbles, the seller/lender can take the property back—at a fraction of the sales value

Prudent sellers and their brokers or attorneys can structure and negotiate the note terms to benefit themselves and still appeal to the buyer/borrower. Most commercial property is financed by banks. In effect, they are the seller's lending competitor. The seller must craft terms to compete with institutional lender. Here's an example.

Suppose an institutional lender requires 30% down and charges a 5% interest rate. The bank may take 60 days to check credit, order, and review an appraisal, underwrite the transaction, and prepare the loan documents. The bank may charge several thousand dollars for fees and appraisal. By contrast, the seller won't charge for an appraisal and can process the paperwork within 10 days. The seller might accept 25% down and charge 5½ or 6% interest.

A prudent seller can structure the note to minimize prepayment risk. A seller may give a longer term than the bank, to stretch out the tax consequences. In the previous example, if lending rates drop from 5% to 4%, the buyer/borrower would want to prepay the loan. Early payment would shift all tax consequences forward. A hefty prepayment penalty can reduce the seller's risk. You and your advisors can structure the loan to protect your interest and still appeal to the buyer.

Sell Your Building, Pay the Taxes, and Move On

A fourth major option is to sell the property, pay the tax, and move forward with a simpler life. A variety of reasons prompt some people to select this option. Some reasons are psychological, and others are financial.

When you sell your property and pay the taxes today, you eliminate the risk of higher tax rates later. Over the past 100 years, income tax rates have gone up and down several times. No one knows what the tax rates will be 5 or 25 years from now. Paying taxes now eliminates that uncertainty. When escrow closes, the sellers have a lot of cash; paying taxes seems less painful. Property values and circumstances will be different in the following years; the seller may or may not have cash later.

Chuck and Jane will choose an option and move on to the next third of life. Their big motivations are to savor more time with family and friends, to travel, and to reap some of the benefits from their decades of hard work. They also have another motivation.

While Chuck and Jane love their children, who are smart and well-educated and have good values, they have a worry, too. While Chuck and Jane have become knowledgeable investors and wealth managers, their children have not. Chuck and Jane can make changes that will make it easier for their children to handle their inheritance without needing to be savvy investors. But, they wonder, "What could we do to make sure that our children are ready for the wealth we will pass to them?" That's what the next chapter is about.

Transferring Your Legacy Wealth

"They who provide much wealth for the children but neglect to improve them in virtue, do like those who feed their horses well, but never train them to be useful."

~ SOCRATES

"Wealth is very dangerous inheritance, unless the inheritor is trained to active benevolence."

~ CHARLES SIMMONS

"Property left to heirs may soon be lost; but the inheritance of virtue—a good name, an unblemished reputation—will abide forever. If those who are toiling to leave their heirs wealth, would but take half the pains to secure for them virtuous habits, how much more serviceable would they be. The largest property could slip away from heirs, but virtue will stand by them to the last."

~ WILLIAM GRAHAM SUMNER

STANFORD PROFESSOR LAURA CARSTENSEN WRITES in her book, *A Long Bright Future*, that most of us will outlive our grandparents by 30 years or more. That means that we can look forward to a longer productive life than any other human beings in history. Even so, sometime in the next 100 years, you and I will be gone. Perhaps those we leave behind will benefit from our being here, and they will be wiser and better people because of our choices. We hope they'll tell good stores about us.

Earlier in the book, I introduced you to Paul and Betty. Their children and many others live better lives because of what they left and the way they lived. Their family and others tell stories about Paul and Betty, both good and bad. Their legacy includes their children, who have become prudent investors and have increased the family's wealth left to them.

This chapter is about passing on your legacy wealth. You'll learn that Paul and Betty's experience is rare, and you'll learn about the three ways investors approach legacy wealth transfer. I'll review the reasons why so few people pass on their wealth effectively and how you can become another exception. You have worked hard to build your wealth, but your heirs could squander it unless you begin to plan more effectively for the inevitable transition and begin now.

Risk: Shirtsleeves to Shirtsleeves in Three Generations

Paul and Betty's experience is a great example of how this can work. In the beginning, they began with love and no money. They started with a single rental property. They added to their holdings while having other businesses and holding other jobs. They later transitioned to managing their properties full time. They passed their property and, more importantly, their *values* to their six children.

Their children were all involved in the apartments. The parents mentored and the kids learned how to be prudent investors and good citizens. Among their family values are compassion, fairness, faith, generosity, and poise. Their surviving daughter phrased one of those values this way:

"Be fair to your fellow human being. You don't know what they've been through." Now the children are involved with the community and their church. Paul and Betty's grandchildren are learning landlording and life lessons from Paul and Betty's children.

Unfortunately, their situation is not the norm. You've probably read or heard about an heir squandering their entire inheritance. The case of Cornelius Vanderbilt is one of the most dramatic.

When Vanderbilt died in 1877, he was the richest person who had ever lived in the United States. Within fifty years of Cornelius's death, one of his descendants died penniless. When more than a hundred of Cornelius's descendants met in 1973, none were millionaires!

The sad Vanderbilt story of wealth melting away is the story of too many families who build wealth. In fact, it's so common that we have a saying about it. The American version is "shirtsleeves to shirtsleeves in three generations." Many other cultures have similar sayings.

The first generation—and maybe that's you—has known hard times and has worked and sacrificed for a better life. By their later years, they can afford a comfortable lifestyle and have assets to pass on to their then-adult children. However, unlike Paul and Betty, many people transfer their wealth but not the virtues and values that helped create the wealth. If the next generation receives the fruit from the trees, but do not pass along the "root system" and "healthy trunk of the tree," the virtues and values that created it, that's where the trouble starts.

The second generation, also maybe you, remembers the parents' sacrifices. They remember harder times and respect the value of hard work and wise investing. They build on what they were given and hand the wealth off to the third generation.

But the third generation, probably not you, never knew hard times. They've known only wealth and haven't seen much sacrifice. Instead, they too often spend their way through their inheritance. They and their children wind up in shirtsleeves. Worst of all, they have no family model of the virtues and values that enabled their grandparents to build wealth.

Wealth manager Roy O. Williams and his partner Vic Preisser became experts in understanding reasons some families remain intact and grow generationally—and why others crumble and disintegrate. They painstakingly researched and interviewed 3,250 families with an average net worth of $20 million. They further studied the nearly 1,000 families of the original 3,250+ where the wealth creators had died and attempted to transfer the wealth and family ties forward. They found that 70% of the time, the family and the wealth did not survive even one generational transfer! And by the second transfer, over 90% of the families and their wealth were no longer intact. "Indeed, 70 percent of wealthy families lose their wealth by the second generation and a stunning 90% by the third."

That sad fact doesn't tell us much about why it happens or how you can do better. To begin to understand that, let's review the common ways people transfer wealth to their heirs.

Three Ways Investors Approach Legacy Wealth Transfer

My experience is that wealthy people have three ways to deal with the transfer of wealth to their heirs. Some don't plan at all; they decide that what happens after they're gone is not their problem. Others attempt to influence or control how the next generation will act. A smaller number intentionally prepare their heirs to manage their inheritance wisely.

Leave it up to fate and the heirs

A surprising number of wealthy people decide that what happens in the next generation is not their problem. They figure that their job is to build the wealth, set the example, and plan the estate so that the maximum amount of wealth passes through probate to their heirs. After that, it's up to the kids.

Sometimes leaving it up to the heirs happens by default. Many but not all of us may have the extra three decades that Laura Carstensen predicts. Heart attacks and accidents take people before they've arranged their affairs. Some people slip into dementia or wasting illness before they put things in order. And some people just keep putting it off until they die.

That is courting disaster. Your heirs can't have the investment savvy you've developed over decades. If they have no experience or knowledge of how to manage wealth, things can get ugly fast. Your heirs could act in two dangerous ways. Perhaps they'll be frozen, like deer in the headlights, or they'll act like every day is their birthday and they suddenly have lots of money to spend.

Drifting, not acting, leaving things up to the heirs, needlessly endangers them and the wealth you've spent a life time accumulating. You've heard that "failing to plan is planning to fail." You can do better. It takes courage and it takes time, but you can do it. You've spent years building your wealth; now finish the job by spending the necessary time to ensure that your work and sacrifice will have the effect you intended.

Consider another common mistake before studying the best way to educate and train your heirs and structure the inheritance so your heirs will maturely administer and develop what you leave.

Try to influence or control the way the next generation will act

Many people hire a smart trust attorney in an attempt to protect the inheritance. They try to limit the risk of their heirs' making terrible mistakes or squandering their parents' hard-earned wealth. One good practice is to tailor the investments to the abilities and inclinations of the heirs.

Perhaps one of your heirs doesn't have the temperament for rental ownership or even for managing any investments. He or she wants investments to be in "set it and forget it" mode and not require attention or involvement. You can use a 1031 exchange to convert your asset to a single-tenant triple-net property.

If your "heir" is a church, synagogue, or charity, your skilled trust attorney can structure your estate to maximize your tax advantages and the nonprofit's ultimate benefit while disinheriting the tax man. Charitable remainder trusts and other vehicles provide many options. Talk to several smart counselors.

Those are effective ways to facilitate transferring wealth to the next generation because they can limit or influence the way those who receive your money will act. Some people attempt to influence the way their heirs will act by regulating the timing and the amount that they pass to their children and grandchildren.

Warren Buffett has some strong and clearly stated ideas about how much of his billions of dollars should pass to his children. In 1986, Buffett told *Fortune* magazine that he didn't believe in giving his children "a lifetime supply of food stamps just because they came out of the right womb." He wants his children to make their own way, and he wants to support them. Buffett thinks that the perfect amount to leave his children is "enough money so that they would feel they could do anything, but not so much that they could do nothing."

Bill and Melinda Gates plan something similar.

Kevin O'Leary is the Canadian entrepreneur known to millions from his appearances on the television shows *Dragon's Den* and *Shark Tank*. He doesn't plan to leave his children *any* of his millions. In 2013, he was interviewed for an article in *Chatelaine* magazine, an English-language Canadian lifestyle magazine, with the largest paid circulation in Canada.

> You want to prepare your children for launching their own lives. I tell wealthy parents that if they don't kick their kids out of the house and put them under the stresses of the real world they will fail to launch—they will become unsuccessful adults. I really believe that. I am setting up generational skipping trusts so I can provide education for their children. They will always be

taken care of. The message is that once school is over, you're out and good luck to you.

If you're a millionaire and don't know what a generation skipping trust is, Google it or ask your CPA or trust attorney.

Most people who attempt to control their heirs' actions do something different than Buffett, Gates, and O'Leary. They hire attorneys to craft complicated trust documents. That may work in theory, but it doesn't always work in practice. Not even the best attorney can consider all the possibilities. Some clever heirs or their attorney may be able to "game the system."

So, while planning is necessary, it isn't sufficient. Planning is most effective when you combine it with intentionally preparing your heirs to manage their inheritance wisely.

Prepare the heirs

A smaller number of wealthy folks invest some of their time and energy to prepare their heirs to be wise stewards of their inheritance. A 2012 U.S. Trust survey found that more than half of wealthy Baby Boomers had not fully disclosed their wealth to their heirs. Thirteen percent had not told the heirs anything about the wealth they would be inheriting.

Preparing your heirs to receive your assets and manage them wisely will not happen automatically. It's something you must work at. It is hard. Remember that everything worthwhile you've ever done was hard. If you didn't have a history of completing the hard things, you would not be reading this book.

The wisest wealthy people I know increase the odds of successful wealth transfer by preparing the inheritance for the heirs and preparing the heirs for wise wealth management. The details vary, but being intentional, preparing the inheritance, and preparing the heirs are always present. Before we consider how this works in real life, though, let's review why intergenerational wealth transfer fails so often.

Why Wealth Transfers Fail

Roy Williams's excellent book, *Love and Money*, has much solid advice about communication, goals, values, and trust. Williams investigated the experience of 3,000+ families over a 20-year period to discover why so many smart, savvy, hard-working people who had built wealth, failed to pass that wealth along.

You might guess that the problem was poor estate planning. But poor legal/tax/investment advice was a factor only 3% of the time. Almost all the time (97%), the problem was in family dynamics. Some families didn't communicate. Others didn't take the time to prepare heirs to manage their inheritance. And others didn't demonstrate and articulate family values that could guide the stewardship of wealth.

That data, along with what we know about how people approach wealth transfer, provides ideas about what to do now to ensure that your life's work—that is, your wealth—will wind up in competent hands when the time comes.

A Better Way

Paul and Betty's family modeled a better way. Compare their method to the factors Roy Williams identified as the most effective intergenerational transfer of values and wealth.

Effective intergenerational transfer of values and wealth begins with the end in mind, a vision of the family legacy.

Failure in family dynamics and values accounts for almost all the failed transfers, but Williams breaks that out into three main reasons:

- Breakdown in family communication and trust
- Failure to establish family values, sometimes called a family mission statement
- Inadequately prepared heirs

Family communication and trust are vital

Williams says that "breakdown in family communication and trust" accounts for 60% of the failures. When Paul and Betty's children were growing up, the parents talked to the children constantly about personal and family matters. Paul and Betty discussed business at the kitchen table and answered their children's questions. Today, those children, now adults, use regular conference calls to continue that kitchen-table experience.

Family values matter

Williams's language is "failure to establish a family mission." Some people might phrase that as "family values," but the idea of mission shows purpose and direction. By whatever name, they account for 12% of the failures. Paul and Betty's children learned what their parents valued in two ways. First, Paul and Betty lived the values; they set the example. Second, they told their children what they believed and why. You need both. Neither setting the example alone nor explaining values alone is adequate.

Preparing the heirs is essential

Williams identifies "inadequately prepared heirs" as the cause of 25% of the failures. Recently, one of our clients expressed his worry this way:

> My kids graduated from colleges that I would've never even considered applying to. They both have Master's degrees and yet they're dumb as a bag of hammers about money. I understood more in junior high about the value of the dollar than my kids and their spouses all put together.

Paul and Betty prepared their children to be wise apartment investors by involving them in the business from an early age. Your heirs are never too young or too old to learn your heart, and your vision. When you involve them in every part of the business, they learn skills and values at the same time.

Make sure they're in the room when you talk to your CPA and investment advisors. Even though you and they may be uncomfortable initially, it is better for them to learn before they make costly mistakes. Encourage them to ask questions. Have a dialogue with them about important things. They can have a say, without necessarily having a vote. Here are a few things you should discuss:

- Why are we investing?
- What is the purpose of wealth?
- Who are we?
- What do we stand for?
- What will we do to close the transaction?
- What won't we do to close the transaction?

Paul and Betty's children are following their parents' example and involving their children in business discussions, including their conference calls. When you involve your heirs in managing your investments, they will make mistakes. Hold them accountable for those mistakes and help them learn from them, so they will grow into courageous and prudent managers of wealth.

Good professional advice is required

Williams ascribes only 3% of failures to "poor legal/tax/investment advice." It is the smallest percentage of wealth transfer failures, but it's still important. The chapter, Team Up with a Great Broker, taught you how to select a top professional adviser. Use the same principles to choose an attorney, CPA, and other advisors. Then investigate a range of options.

Many wealthy people use charitable remainder trusts, a personal foundation, a family limited partnership, or similar vehicles to accomplish their legacy wealth transfer goals. Libraries are written on these topics. These estate planning and asset management tools can enable you to accomplish several goals. While you're alive you can provide income for the balance of your heirs' lives, retain control or influence, involve and/or train and maybe even pay heirs, reduce taxes, and move assets to the people and or charities of your choice. After you've passed, your estate planning will influence the heirs and how the assets are deployed.

Each tool has different benefits and quirks. Some people are charitably minded; others, not so much. You can buy life insurance to replace much or all the wealth if the owner wants to both donate and also provide for family. Thousands of trust attorneys and wealth managers can provide appropriate, customized, and confidential counseling on these important topics.

As you work through the process described in this book, you will be better prepared than most people to make wise decisions about wealth transfer. You will have learned to select wise advisors and clarified your personal values. You will have applied those values to analyzing many opportunities and deciding when and where to invest.

Your Investment Life Trajectory Summary

FOR MORE DETAILS about any of the following highlights, see the chapter indicated in parentheses.

If you want to build wealth and keep your capital working, you have two superior options. You can sell the building and buy another property, or you can refinance and use the cash as a down payment for the next purchase. (Prolonging Your Capital's Growth Spurt)

Trading up is the core strategy that most clients use to build legacy wealth, but refinancing is sometimes a better choice. Your great broker can help you decide when refinancing is a better strategy. (Prolonging Your Capital's Growth Spurt)

Apartment investing is a wonderful way to build legacy wealth, but eventually you may want to move on. Perhaps you'll get enough of tenants, trash, and toilets, or you may decide that higher cash flow and no management or maintenance is better than chasing appreciation. (Moving On)

There are four common options for those who want to move on, and trade-offs go with each one. You can exchange your equity for NNN or another commercial property type; you can sell your property and carry the mortgage; or you can sell your property, pay the taxes, and get on with life. (Moving On)

Single-tenant triple-net (NNN) properties are the lowest-risk investment real estate. *Single tenant* means that only one business leases the property. *Triple net* means the landlord receives a check net of taxes, net of insurance costs, and net of all other property-related costs. A 1031 exchange enables you to sell your apartments and purchase an NNN property without paying a third of your profit in taxes. (Moving On)

With NNN property, a large chunk of your wealth is in a single asset. The tenant's high credit reduces the need for diversification. NNN's main benefit is the low-risk, "almost no management–almost no worry" income. (Moving On)

Other commercial properties are larger assets, rented to multiple business tenants for multiyear terms. It takes more capital to operate bigger assets that have higher tenant turnover costs. During recessions, vacancies take longer to fill than would be true of multifamily properties.

Instead of moving all your equity into a different property, you can carry the mortgage on the sale of property that you currently own. You will need to structure loan terms to compete with banks and structure the note to minimize prepayment risk. (Moving On)

Sometimes people have psychological and financial reasons for choosing to simply sell their apartments, pay the taxes, and move on. (Moving On)

Many people work hard and sacrifice to build wealth. But research indicates that the odds are against your wealth surviving even one generation unless you wisely prepare your heirs for wealth. (Transferring Your Legacy Wealth)

Some people keep the assets till they pass and let the heirs decide what to do with them. Drifting, not acting, leaving things up to the heirs, needlessly endangers them and the wealth you've spent a lifetime accumulating. (Transferring Your Legacy Wealth)

Bad investment or legal advice causes just 3% of wealth transfer failures. The other 97% results from a combination of poor communication, unclear goals, and failure to prepare the heirs to be prudent managers of the wealth they receive. (Transferring Your Legacy Wealth)

To increase the odds that your hard-earned wealth will benefit your heirs for decades, pursue an integrated strategy of wealth transfer. Set the example of prudent wealth management, involve your heirs in the wealth management process, and explain your process and decisions to teach your heirs important lessons. (Transferring Your Legacy Wealth)

Moving on is the final step in your apartment-investing journey. We'll look at the entire journey and some important lessons in the conclusion that awaits you in the following pages.

Conclusion

"There are two things to aim for in life: first, to get
what you want; and, after that, to enjoy it. Only the wisest
of mankind achieve the second."
~ LOGAN PEARSALL SMITH

"What you would do, begin it. For boldness has wonder,
power, and magic in it."
~ GOETHE

WHEN PAUL AND BETTY MARRIED, they had character but no assets.
About 5 years later, with his mom, they bought a single property. With
passing time, they bought more. In the beginning, they had "day jobs" and
worked on their properties in what could have been spare time. Eventually,
they managed their properties full time and involved all their children in
the management, maintenance, and decision making. It's an inspiring story.

Their children learned emotional intelligence and became savvy
apartment investors and fine people. They manage many properties, often

in partnerships with each other. They involve their own children in the process. Paul and Betty's children are now apartment and commercial property owners and model emotional intelligence and other family values to their kids.

This multigenerational story illustrates an important message: Apartment investing is more than a wealth-building tool; it can also help transmit your values.

This book represents gleanings from a generation of investors who live lives worth imitating. You've been exposed to techniques that can make your money multiply, and you've received some nudges to grow into the person you were created to be. Here are the key lessons you might apply.

Many people build wealth quietly, the way Paul and Betty did. I hope you'll review the principles of wealthy thinking that quiet millionaires use to build their wealth.

Investors who remain calm in the face of provocation or bad luck are more likely to get the best deals. Emotional intelligence is a continuous challenge for many of us. May this book improve your skills faster than I improved mine. Remember: You can have your say or you can have your way, but only having your way builds wealth.

Your success will come faster if you prepare before investing. Get your finances in order first. Team up with a great broker and develop strong and repeatable investing processes. Clarify your personal priorities and learn the market.

The best investors are disciplined; they do the little things right to make sure the big things work. It's hard to be a good investor, but it's also hard to reach the end of your life without the resources to live well, too. Pick your hard.

You and your broker will routinely repeat the wealth escalator process as you build your legacy wealth. The basic process is simple and proven. More than 50 years ago, William Nickerson wrote the first income property classic, currently titled, *How I Turned $1,000 into Five Million in*

Real Estate in My Spare Time. His strategy still works. Buy "the dog on the block," a property with the right things wrong with it. Improve it, sell it for a profit, and repeat the process.

Our team has helped clients win with this core strategy for a generation. We developed and refined some simple systems to improve the process. One of our systems prioritizes opportunities. It evaluates and ranks opportunities to clarify which one is your best fit.

Too many brokers and investors waste time chasing "the one best deal." That's a poor strategy for two reasons. First, your objective isn't to get a near-perfect deal, it's to close a superior opportunity from the available options. Second, the multiple-offers strategy is the surest and quickest way to capture a better opportunity. Writing backup offers also increases your odds. Remember, great investors have a bias for action, a willingness to explore options, and the determination to close.

Landlording, human-scale capitalism, offers you many options to build legacy. Your desired legacy should drive your decisions about who will handle property management and maintenance, setting rents, and improving your property's value. Paul and Betty's children learned about fairness and dealing with difficult people by watching their parents manage their properties and deal with flawed people, including tenants and vendors.

Successful apartment investors' bias for action also enables you to recognize when it's time to sell an asset. Our most successful clients review their holdings regularly and seek opportunities to trade up. Cash from the sale of one building provides the down payment for the next wealth-building acquisition. Cash, not merely wealth, is needed for a down payment.

IRS section 1031 allows real estate investors to defer taxes. This powerful tax benefit enables you to use all the sale proceeds to trade up, while deferring taxes legally. Under current tax law, your heirs receive property at date-of-death value, meaning you may effectively disinherit the tax man. A 1031 exchange is like an interest-free loan from the government, and you may never have to repay it.

Apartment investing is a superior way to build legacy wealth, but eventually you may want to move on. If you make that decision, you have some common options. A 1031 exchange enables larger trade-ups or moves into NNN or a different property type. You can carry the mortgage and slow the tax obligation. Or, you can sell your property, pay the taxes, and get on with life. Trade-offs come with each option.

Many of our clients have better educations than their parents, so their income is higher. They use part of their high income as the seed corn for their apartment investing. Other clients earn wealth from other endeavors and use apartment investing to grow it further. Our clients are different in many ways, but they share two things: They worked hard to build their wealth, and they want their heirs to reap the benefits. That doesn't happen automatically. Too few fortunes survive until the third generation.

The vast majority of those wealth-transfer failures result from poor communication, unclear goals, and failure to prepare the heirs to manage their wealth effectively. The good news is that you can triumph over those issues by following Paul and Betty's example.

Successfully transferring wealth to the next generation works better when you involve your heirs in building wealth, so they will become prudent investors. Your heirs have a better chance to learn and maybe have your values. Also, you will learn about your heirs, so you can structure the inheritance to fit their preferences and strengths.

I'm a voracious reader, and I've spent most of my adult life reading about how to be better and trying to apply what I've learned. So I was appalled to learn that few people buy a book and read it all the way through, and even fewer put what they've learned to work.

My sincere hope is that you're reading this volume because you're the exception. Our clients' outrageous success suggests that you, too, can build wealth and live a life worth emulating when you use these tools and techniques. Please put them to work. You can become a good investor, even though you're not a natural one, if you engage in a version of deliberate practice.

Malcolm Gladwell popularized the work of psychology researcher K. Anders Ericsson regarding the way human beings build mastery at anything, including apartment investing. Gladwell said that mastery requires 10,000 hours of deliberate practice. Deliberate practice is more than simply putting in time; it's focused, intentional work to get better.

Deliberate practice means trying to master the things that currently exceed your capacity. It's a lot of time fumbling, stumbling, being frustrated, getting it mostly wrong and partially right, and then eventually getting it right most of the time. Learning is uncomfortable. A mentor said, "If you're green, you're growing; if you're ripe, you're rotting." Novices practice until they can get it right. Masters practice until they can't get it wrong.

Commitment to excellence involves facing the reality of our mediocre performance and then deciding to make the commitment and following through on that commitment to master the things that baffle us. I hate feeling like an idiot. However, if I'm going to serve my team and my clients better, if I'm going to show the love to Sandy in the ways that matter to her, I must get a lot better at things I'm not worth a flip at now.

To become a master, get comfortable with being uncomfortable. I have some tendencies that impair my ability to serve others well. I have a well-rehearsed story I tell myself that my current performance is pretty good. It's really hard for me to smash some of my mediocre habits and transform myself into the better person I aspire to become. *Really* hard? Make that *damned* hard!

Don't hear what I'm not saying. This is not a call to be Superman in all fields; it's an invitation to be explicit about what matters to you. What few things are essential to you, and what many things can be good enough? "Good enough" is good enough for most of what you and I do.

Candidly, "pretty good" American real estate investors can become millionaires and amass more than enough material resources to provide for their households and leave a tidy nest egg for those who follow. We don't have to become Bill Gates or Warren Buffett to have an immense beneficial impact on the people around us.

Paul and Betty didn't start out knowing how to be landlords or successful property investors. They had to learn. Mark and Sharon's story is similar. My clients who made money in another field still had to learn how apartment investing works. They all had to master the craft, and so they all were uncomfortable and they all made mistakes along the way. If you master this craft, you will do the same.

You've already demonstrated that you have the right stuff by buying this book and reading it. Bravo! I want to give you a gift to reward you for what you've done so far and to encourage you to put this book to work. A bookplate is a piece of paper or label that you insert or paste at the front of a book. Today, authors use them to "autograph" books at a distance. I will send you a free, signed bookplate if you send me your postal address using the contact form on the website for this book.

You'll make your own choice about how much emotional and time cost you will pay to attain your goals, material and otherwise. You will pick your hard.

Nothing in this book is beyond you. The most successful investors I work with weren't born with a special investing gene. They are ordinary people who decided what was important to them and then committed to learning and trying and learning and trying to do the things that would make their life a life worth imitating. You can do that, too.

Every book has a hero. If you take these lessons and use them to build your wealth and your legacy, the hero will be you.

Appendices

Appendix A

Supply and Demand

MOST INVESTORS BUY RENTALS located within an hour of their home or work. That seems to be about the maximum distance you can go and make face-to-face capitalism work. You may live in one of the few markets that offer huge potential with limited risk. On the other hand, you may live in a market with immense risk and limited potential for investing profitably in apartments.

Supply-and-demand factors have far more influence on future values than most rental owners understand. A great operator may do only adequately in a poor market, while a mediocre investor does far better in a great market. Great markets are great because they are *supply constrained*.

In supply-constrained markets, there is a steady demand for new and improved rental housing, but government or topography or both significantly restrict new construction. For example, in the past 30 years, San Diego has built about half as much multifamily housing as the population growth needed. San Diego and a few other supply-constrained markets, maybe 10–15% of the nation, are wealth escalators where even drunken fools have become millionaires.

West Coast cities, New York, Washington, DC, and cities that perceive themselves to be environmentally minded are disproportionately supply constrained. Many investors in those markets buy based on next year's potential income, not current income. Supply-constrained markets offer the potential to monetize substantial rent increases. This financial power tool does not work well in ordinary or shrinking markets.

Maybe half the markets are ordinary. There, both population and jobs are growing and there are no significant restrictions on new construction. "Developer Dan" can go to the fringe of the community and buy some dirt, and within 9 months apartments are built and leasing agents are offering move-in specials. Once a decade or so, the market gets overbuilt. Then it usually takes a year or more for the market to absorb the excess apartments.

Maybe a third of the markets have supply-and-demand factors that almost eliminate appreciation potential. Many Rust Belt cities and small farming communities are in this category. The population is either shrinking or the number of renters is growing slower than either the national average or the population of the metropolitan statistical area.

Property in supply-constrained markets costs more than similar property in the other market types. San Diego apartments can cost 3 to 7 times as much as apartments in Texas, North Carolina, or Florida, or 5 to 10 times as much as Rust Belt apartments.

Ten thousand dollar renovations may be justified when the rents can be raised $1,200 annually, but not make sense when the rental income only climbs $300 annually. Costs for an apartment full of appliances or a set of cabinets or new flooring do not vary much, state to state. However, a 200-mile difference might mean the difference between apartments costing $50,000 or apartments costing $250,000. The great broker you partner with will be your best guide to the strategies that work best where you invest.

Appendix B

Are You Ready to Invest?

IF YOU'RE A NOVICE OR APPRENTICE, you must assess whether you are financially fit enough to handle the program for building legacy wealth that you'll find in this book. It would be nice if those infomercials and get-rich-quick-and-easy promises were true, but they're not. You can't start with just a good attitude and discipline and expect to succeed.

It's like climbing a mountain. Before you start your climb, you must be sure you're fit enough. Before I climbed Mount Kilimanjaro, I put in months of preparation, including diet, exercise, and rigorous training hikes. We all had to receive a physician's authorization that we were fit enough, before we made the climb. Here's how to gauge whether you're fiscally fit enough for apartment investing.

Do You Have Enough Cash?

You need cash for down payments and repairs. With enough cash, you can seize opportunities. Each year I discover great opportunities that won't be on the market for long. When I do, I tell some of the investors I work with about them. Their having cash lets them jump into action before someone else grabs the opportunity. Investors who are prepared have cash and the courage to capture superb opportunities while others are evaluating the option and before most people even know about the possibility.

The amount you'll need for a down payment will vary by market. In San Diego, as I write this, the minimum to invest in apartments is $200K. Your broker can give you guidelines for your market.

When your strategy is building wealth, the basic process is to choose properties with the right things wrong with them and then fix those things. That's how you can increase the rents and build value. The investors who sell the improved asset for a profit have *monetized the increase*—financial speak for *taken their profit*—and they can use the larger stack of cash to buy another property with the right things wrong with it. In San Diego, clients need $200K cash or $500K in equity in other income property they are willing to sell and redeploy.

Buying the asset is the first step. The most successful investors upgrade the asset, which takes some extra capital. Prudent investors also have an additional cash cushion, which the lender will want to see and which sometimes will be needed.

Some lenders may require enough cash to make 6 months' mortgage payments in addition to your down payment and repair funds. Cash is only one part of the puzzle.

Do You Have a Clean Balance Sheet?

Successful investors are prudent risk takers. There is dynamic tension. Successful investors and entrepreneurs take risks, but they don't take unnecessary risks. Prudence prepares for inevitable life surprises. Job loss happens. Health crises, accidents, and natural disasters happen. You can't predict them, but you must be ready for them.

Don't consider investing in apartments until you've paid off your credit card debt. I suggest paying off any car loans, too. The less debt and the more ready cash you have, the safer you are from life's surprises and the greater your ability to seize the opportunities life and your broker will send your way.

If you're fiscally fit enough to build your legacy wealth, congratulations! Now is a good time to start. On the other hand, if your finances aren't where they need to be for prudent investing, you'd be wise to become fiscally fit before challenging better-prepared competitors.

Appendix C

Due Diligence

"Trust but verify" is an old Russian proverb. It was President Reagan's approach when it came to enforcing treaties with our Cold War adversary. It's good advice for apartment investors when working through the due-diligence process.

An Outline of the Due-Diligence Process

The due-diligence process begins when the buyer and the seller have agreed upon basic price and terms. At that point, both parties have made some assumptions about the property and about the ability of the other party to complete the transaction. During due diligence, both parties share relevant information and the buyer tests the validity of their assumptions.

Your experienced broker has been through this process dozens or maybe hundreds of times and can help you understand what's required. You will learn to be a better investor and teammate if you ask questions about anything you don't understand.

Both sides have a vested interest in either closing the transaction according to an agreed-upon schedule or, if the transaction will not close, then getting loose quickly to find a more suitable result. The California Association of Realtors® (CAR) has created a complete and fair contract which is not slanted to either side. Many state Realtors® associations have similar contracts. The 2018 CAR contract has a default setting of 17 days for all due diligence except for that which is related to the loan. That is ample time to review all the documents, inspect the building, and answer almost all the questions that arise during this investigation period.

If the truth does not match the buyer's expectations, then the buyer can cancel within that time frame and escrow will refund the earnest money. Sometimes the results are not what the buyer expected, and buyer and seller will negotiate some middle ground that moves the sale forward. However, once the buyer has waived contingencies, the negotiations are complete.

In San Diego County, perhaps a third of escrows fail. Some failures are because the property did not meet the buyer's expectations and a satisfactory adjustment could not be made. Other times it is because one of the principals or one of the agents blundered. Many mistakes can be corrected, explained, or apologized for, and the transaction can still go forward. Ego and deceit are harder to work around.

Title Insurance

Each state has its own protocol. In California, the seller buys title insurance to protect the buyer for the full purchase amount. Most income properties have a loan. The buyer/borrower, pays for the title insurance to protect the lender for the loan amount. The seller pays a higher rate, and the borrower pays a lower rate. Few buyers pay for a surveyor to mark the edges of the property and provide a new map with all the measurements.

Your broker can tell you the standard practice in your market.

The process looks different if you are buying or if you are selling. Let's look at the seller's side first, because that will give you an idea of what to expect and ask for when you are the buyer. The information is for San Diego County, California, as I write this in 2018. Be sure to have your broker review it for additions, deletions, and modifications to fit your particular situation.

When You Are the Seller

When you are selling, do not give the buyer an excuse to go away, and do everything you can to help them complete their due diligence and approve their purchase expeditiously. Remember the old adage, "Time kills deals." Delays frustrate the buyer, who may decide your deal wasn't worth it after all. Provide the following to the buyer as quickly as possible. Some items may require repairs or other work on the building.

Copies of books and records

Current rent roll should match the leases or rental agreements for all occupied units, including any addendums and rent-increase notices. Rental applications are not usually provided in California. In other states buyers may be able to review them. Residents' social security numbers and credit information are appropriate for the owner to see, but not potential buyers.

Here are additional information lender and or buyer will expect:

- Income and expense statements (Schedule E from Tax Return) for the previous 2 years, plus year-to-date. It is becoming increasingly commonplace for buyers to ask for the most current "12 Months Trailing Operating Statement," formatted with monthly subtotals. Be prepared to provide this, and you might even consider making it your standard.

- Service agreements and contracts such as:

  - Landscaping maintenance

  - Laundry lease

  - Pest control

- Pool cleaning
- Trash collection

- Personal property list (number of stoves, refrigerators, etc., that transfer to the buyer.)

- Insurance loss run—insurance company's report on payout concerning property over the previous 5 years

- Most recent 3 months' invoices for gas, electric, water, sewer, and trash

- List of capital improvements completed to the property within last three years

Lenders will often request that income/expense reports, as well as rent roll, be signed and dated by the seller.

The buyer needs the income and expense statements and rent roll to submit a completed loan application package. It is critical that the books and records are available early in the process to avoid unnecessary delays. If the seller expects the buyer to submit the loan application within 5 days of acceptance, the seller needs to provide all the necessary property information within 3 days of acceptance.

Pest control report

In most transactions in San Diego, the seller pays for the termite inspection report. If that is the case for you, decide which company you will get to do the inspection and tell your broker. He or she may be able to get you a discount on the inspection fee or on a warranty. Many owners don't like to disturb residents twice, once for pest control and then again for the buyer inspection.

Some effective brokers encourage the seller to obtain a pest control report immediately upon listing. The advantage of this timing is that the seller and broker know the truth early. They can frame the buyers' expectations, saying the property is listed for *only* this price because there is modest infestation. It seems that 95% of California buildings have some termites. One of my clients was a world-renowned entomologist, an insect scientist. He said in San Diego most dry-wood termite colonies die before the building integrity is severely compromised. Few buyers tent the structure, even if they obtain some discount for property condition. Sellers almost never tent apartment buildings. Lenders force that cost onto home buyers. Apartment investors find lenders who don't require that superfluous cost.

If the pest control report is not done before the physical inspection, then do it during the buyer's inspection. If the first buyer does not go ahead with the transaction, you can use the same report for subsequent buyers.

Expect that there will be some termite infestation. The termite companies usually recommend tenting the entire building. In most escrows for properties five units and larger, the seller does not do any pest control work, but often will make some token concession. Since the apartment buyer makes a substantial down payment, most lenders will fund without any pest control clearance. Alternatively, lenders are more likely to insist on termite clearance for four units and below. Those loans have a lower down payment, higher loan to value, and thus a higher risk than lower loan to value.

"Local" treatment involves spraying poison where infestation can be seen. Often the termite nest is out of sight. I estimate that fewer than 20% of the apartment transactions in San Diego have even local treatment within a year of closing.

Also inspected as part of the pest control report are dry rot, wet rot, and any earth-to-wood contacts. Dry and wet rot occur most frequently in kitchens and baths near water sources. Some examples where rotting may occur are under sinks, tubs, surrounding tub areas, shower pans, surrounding shower areas, toilets, and floors.

Some cities have special requirements (water conservation, fire protection, earthquake safety). Your expert broker can guide you through what the local jurisdiction needs. California requires sellers to make extra disclosures on one- to four-unit properties.

California mandates: smoke and carbon monoxide detectors and water heater strapping

California law requires smoke and carbon monoxide detectors and that water heaters be strapped to studs to minimize horizontal movement in the event of an earthquake. State law is in effect, even if the contract specifies that sale "as is." California sellers will be asked to certify that the building is in compliance with state law and local ordinance regarding both the water heaters and smoke detectors. It's prudent and simpler to have the building in compliance before the buyer's inspection.

When the buyer notices that the seller has taken care of the little details, he or she is more comfortable about the hard-to-verify items. Alternatively, if the buyer realizes that the seller is skimping on the tiny costs, the buyer may be anxious about the larger-ticket items.

Your parents probably told you about the power of a first impression. A host of psychological research confirms their wisdom. When you sell a property, your first impression is your speed to share information and the way you handle the first details the buyer will see. Do those things right so that the entire process becomes easier. If you leave the impression that you are hard to deal with or that you do slipshod work, the buyer will look harder at the building or may go away.

Local requirements: plumbing retrofit in some San Diego County cities

Your jurisdiction may have special requirements that don't pertain to the rest of nation.

A few cities in San Diego County require that plumbing fixtures meet current water-conservation standards. For example, San Diego and Del Mar ordinances specify that the seller install water-saving toilets, faucets, and showerheads. Since the seller will pay for them anyway, the owner should install them now and begin enjoying the savings. Sometimes the local water provider offers rebates.

If an owner sells the building "as is," the buyer can accept responsibility for the water-conservation retrofit. That small extra cost makes the property less appealing, and the buyer will expect a price concession.

When You Are the Buyer

When you're the buyer, the process is reversed. Now you want to carefully investigate everything to determine if the building is in the condition you expect and to identify exceptions that should merit a concession.

Review the property documents

Look at the books and records and at the leases. Check all the paperwork. Ask for copies of any and all reports the seller may have had performed on the property, including copies of any and all reports that previous potential buyers completed and provided copies of. A 2017 California court decision imposes extra liability on the seller and the broker for information they possess. A 50-year-old building in San Diego County may have had 10 owners. Therefore, most San Diego sellers won't have a building's "as built" plans or other reports that are common in markets with lower turnover and larger assets.

Here are some questions to ask about the property title. Your broker may suggest other questions.

- Can the seller deliver clear title? Are there easements other than routine utility access? An excellent broker should help you interpret this report. If you have questions about the title, the title officer can answer questions about the detail but won't provide legal advice about the significance of issues. The lender is usually a reliable backstop. If there were a big problem, the lender would demand that it be cleared so the mortgage/trust deed would be recorded first, ahead of any other obligations.

- Ensure that there are no covenants, conditions, or restrictions, CC&Rs that would impede your desired use of property. Some properties are restricted to renting only to people over 62 or to disabled persons. A few buildings may have restrictions on rent levels.

- The new lender will insist that all previous liens be cleared as a condition of obtaining a new loan.

- Often the rent roll and leases don't match. People may have moved within the building. The original leases may show old rent amounts. Roommates may have changed. Be sure that documents match current reality.

Review the financials

Review the financials to determine if they are as the seller represented and in line with your assumptions. The buyer's goal in reviewing and studying the financials is not to catch the seller with a "gotcha," but rather to obtain a clear and accurate picture of how much rental income the property is currently generating, and how much it is costing to operate it. The difference between these two numbers is the net operating income, or NOI. People buy income property for income. For properties above $2 million in value, the NOI and cap rate, are the most important indicators of value.

You want to make sure that the NOI you determine will support the sales price you agreed to pay. If it turns out that the NOI is significantly less than what the seller represented, then you have a reason to try to renegotiate the price. Remember that not every rental owner reports all their rents, all their laundry or other vending income. Understand that profit-oriented people don't always pay all taxes. Don't be surprised when income two years ago was lower than now. Rents increase in most buildings, most years. Also keep your BS detector engaged. Less than 5% difference could be understandable, more than 10% probably should set off alarm bells. The Highway Patrol may not pull someone over for 10 mph above the limit, but will for 25 mph above the limit.

Your great broker can help you interpret the financials. There are no dumb questions. Ensure that you understand what the financials are telling you.

Some owners do lots of work on their own, and so the labor and maintenance cost can be low. Alternatively, many owners use their building to smooth their taxable income. When other income is especially good, they seize the opportunity to make repairs. When other income is lean, then the owner spends less for flooring, appliances, paint, etc. Many owners write off repairs against ordinary income. The property value climbs. When they sell, any taxes will be at a lower capital gains rate. Many owners' expense items that IRS might prefer to call capital improvements. That saves owners money on their income taxes.

The seller may have done a terrible job of managing the property. Just because the other fellow spent twice as much for painting or plumbing as you would does not mean the building is a disaster. It means that your efficiency will enable you to profit from your knowledge. A seller's stupidity does not mean the building is a loser. A bad financial history may mean a lower loan and thus a higher down payment. However, being able to quickly boost profitability could signal a superior opportunity.

When you see something outside your expectations, smile and ask. Sometimes you learn a lot by listening. My wise mentor says: "You don't show intelligence by what you say, but by what you ask." Common topics to ask about include:

- Rents
- Vacancy rate
- Expenses

Inspect the property

Go look at the property *and inspect every unit, inside and out*. If it looks like a dump on the outside, it will probably look like a dump on the inside. If looks terrific on the outside, we hope it's going to look terrific on the inside.

Unless you are a general contractor, *hire an inspector who is competent at apartment inspections.* Insurance is a cost of doing business. The inspection is insurance, and it is also a terrific bargaining tool. It will lend credibility to any problems you may find, and it will assist you in negotiating any resulting repairs or price concessions.

In San Diego, one of the best inspectors charges $1,000–$1,500 to inspect a 5-to–12-unit building. The best inspector I know produces a report that's about 20 pages, including:

- Pictures
- A review of the condition of individual units
- Details about the key building components and systems, including the foundation, electrical, plumbing, and roof
- Rough estimates of how much money would be needed over the next 5 years to correct the inevitable deferred maintenance

Prepare for added loan costs

In San Diego County, 90% of the multifamily parcels are less than 16 units. In many other major markets, there are far fewer relatively small investments. Some markets consider a 50-unit building to be a small loan. In San Diego, the vast majority of loans are made by banks and credit unions. Banks and credit unions require less due diligence, that is, third-party reports, for smaller loans. Few have FNMA or Freddie Mac guarantees.

When loans exceed $2 million, lenders are more likely to insist on reports for environmental condition, and a property assessment. These may be used to assess asbestos, energy use, foundation, roofs, and risk of earthquake, flooding, mold, and or soils contamination. The buyer pays for the reports that lenders require.

What to Do with What You Find

No matter which side you're on, the due diligence process usually identifies some things about the building or the other party that surprise you. Generally, the buyer and his broker will use the third-party expert report to bargain for repairs or price concessions. If the seller rejects the first buyer, that does not solve the mechanical deficiency. California law tends toward the weaker party, and in real estate that is the buyer. Sellers have an obligation to reveal "material facts." Once the seller becomes aware of a problem, the seller has an obligation to disclose that to all potential buyers. States east of the Mississippi River tend to have more of a buyer-beware culture. Let your broker be your guide.

Often a skillful broker can obtain a concession far in excess of the inspection cost and offset the financial cost of the deferred maintenance.

Sometimes your own inspection or the inspector's report identifies important things that you didn't expect, like a leaky roof, massive mold, or drug or other illegal activity, and you may cancel the deal and run as fast as you can in the opposite direction.

When you cancel the deal within the contingency period, your broker simply notifies the listing broker, "Thank you very much. Not my client's deal." Make sure this notice is done in writing and within the time limit specified in the contract. The California Association of Realtors, CAR, contract is most commonly used in San Diego. It is a relatively thorough, balanced, and effective form. In California, there are about 20 "fill in the blank" forms, one of which is a cancellation form.

In many markets, the state association of Realtors form is not the standard. Many states have purchase and sale contracts drawn by attorneys. Custom contracts and the attorney time can be dramatically more expensive. My wife and I bought and sold apartments in North Carolina. Our legal costs exceeded 2% of the transaction. Those extra costs added no value above what could have been done by competent brokers working in San Diego without any attorneys.

Your broker will know the local protocol. If you need to cancel, ensure that your cancellation is transmitted appropriately for your contract. For example, in some markets a cancellation notice is given via e-mail, but some sales contracts do not recognize a written e-mail communication as acceptable, or they don't consider it "delivered" until the next day. That will cause a major problem if you or your broker e-mail your cancellation to the seller on the last day of the due-diligence period, and the contract says that the notice is not official until the next day.

When you cancel the contract, the seller does not get to approve your reason. Escrow gives your money back. In hundreds of escrows, I've not yet seen a buyer lose escrow money if the cancellation notice is given properly and within the time limit specified in the purchase contract.

Appendix D

Loans: How Lenders Determine the Amount They'll Lend

MOST INVESTORS BUY APARTMENTS with a loan.

If you can obtain a loan for five units or more and you are a reasonably competent operator, the property will probably be able to make the payment and give you cash flow. The institutional lender builds in plenty of cushion. During an ordinary recession, the property should still be able to make the loan payments. If the value of the property slips sometime during your ownership, the lender does not care, as long as you continue to make the payments.

One of my smartest friends was afraid to buy income property because he did not understand that lenders would force caution on all borrowers. In effect, the lender makes it difficult for an ordinary borrower to get a loan bigger than the property can support.

Most investors want to obtain the maximum loan possible, and that amount is determined by the lender. Once you understand how the lenders calculate the loan, you can focus your time and attention on the opportunities and minimize the wasted effort of chasing buildings that are currently beyond your reach.

Lenders are more conservative than the seller or listing broker and probably even more conservative than the buyer. You can make wiser choices when you understand the assumptions and reasoning behind lenders' vacancy rates, expense numbers, and reserve or capital expense figures. Your assumptions are likely to be different. You probably expect rents to increase, but lenders don't assume that. You hope that you'll do better than average. Lenders work cautiously, based on the average borrower.

Lenders force prudence on the market. They hide the punch bowl when the party gets too wild. When lenders lend less money, buyers must make larger down payments. The higher down payments are the market's way of saying to buyers, "Put your money where your mouth is." In effect, the investors with the cash and courage to commit are the ones who drive the prices. Sellers wish for all their property to be worth twice as much. Lenders want all the prudent loans they can make and don't want to make any bad loans. Thus, appraisers play a critical role.

Lenders hire appraisers to be the prudent, disinterested experts. The appraisers are the sentries who guard against irrational expectations. Sellers always want the maximum price. Brokers love to close and collect a commission, the higher the better. Loan agents are compensated and evaluated for the loans that they make. Many buyers will pay a high price since the bulk of the money comes from the lender. The appraisers help everyone tailor expectations to reality. Appraisers are hired to give a disinterested opinion. They are not God, and they don't set value; instead they provide an opinion. Buyers and sellers also have opinions. If the buyer's opinion exceeds that of the appraiser, the buyer can literally put his money (extra down payment) where his mouth is. It is legal to pay more than the appraisal; it simply takes a bigger down payment.

Lenders might lend the lowest of 75% (or some other percentage they select) of contract value or appraisal or the debt coverage ratio (DCR). For residential property and for small apartments (fourplex or less), the lender will evaluate your ability to repay the loan by reviewing your income and credit standing. If you're seeking a loan for a vacation home, they don't care if you intend to rent it out for a portion of the year to produce some income. They only consider whether you can make the mortgage payments, based on your income and credit standing. Federal law mandates a different underwriting standard for loans to buy investment property of five units or more. Let's review how that works.

For buildings above four units, the lender focuses on the lower of current or projected income from the asset. The math behind the lenders assumptions is based on thousands of income property loans. Lenders who are too lax make bad loans and may get wiped out. Lenders who are too conservative don't make many loans and are not a factor in the market. The organizations that fund transactions are the ones who govern the pace of the market and heavily influence the total volume of transactions.

Generally, the lender will want the property with an ordinary borrower, not a superstar operator, to have $115 to $125 of cash flow to cover every $100 of mortgage payment. Banks call this relationship the debt coverage ratio (DCR). They want a cushion for when things don't go as planned. Lenders will set the loan amount using the most conservative of several methods, including percentage of down payment, relation to replacement cost, or value of comparable buildings. In San Diego and most other supply-constrained markets, the DCR will be most important in determining the loan amount.

The following chart illustrates how a loan underwriter calculates his offer to lend money. It's based on common practice in San Diego County, California, as I write this book in 2018. Your broker will help you adjust to the current situation in your market. The example is for a 10-unit building.

DEBT COVERAGE RATIO MATH		
Gross scheduled income (GSI) ~ potential income	100%	$100,000
Minus at least 5% for vacancies and credit loss	5%	− $5,000
Gross operating income ~ estimated collections	95%	= $95,000
Property taxes*	1.1% of pur-chase price	$14,000
Plus all other cash operating expenses**	$3,000 per unit	+ $30,000
Estimated total expenses		= $44,000
Net operating income	51% of GSI	$51,000
Minus reserves for capital improvements	$250 per unit	− $2,500
Cash available for debt service (lender considers this to be 1.2 times the lender-cushion value)		= $48,500
Value recalculated for lender cushion	divide by 1.2	$40,417

The annual debt service shows maximum loan payment a lender will allow. The current rate tells how much debt that payment can support.

Loan amount is determined by current interest rate; the higher the interest, the lower the loan amount.

*Each state has its own way of determining property tax. In California, it is based on purchase price. Most states have periodic assessments: annually or every 4 or 8 years.

**Your excellent broker or property manager can help you estimate costs in your area.

Lenders typically only care about current income, even when they recognize that rents are far below the market.

Underwriters will use a conservative estimate of the local vacancy, credit loss, and concessions rate, but rarely less than 5% vacancy to calculate their estimate of collections and thus the gross operating income. For example, if the seller collected 98% of the scheduled income, the lender would assume that the next buyer could only collect 95% of scheduled income.

Next, they will deduct property taxes and other operating expenses. Property taxes are determined differently in different jurisdictions. Your broker will know the rates for your area. Operating expenses include both fixed and variable expenses. Fixed expenses will include taxes, fees, insurance, and management. Variable can include utilities, repairs, and other expenses involved in operating property. After deducting the probable expenses, the underwriter will have an estimate of net operating income. That figure will routinely be lower than what the buyer hopes for and further below what the listing broker promoted.

The lender will put in some further cushion. Over the next 30 years, the property will need appliances, heating and cooling equipment, painting, roof replacement, stair and landing repairs, water heater, windows, and so forth. Expect the lender to budget about $250 per unit per year. Few owners set aside a separate saving account or sinking fund for those items, but the lender will underwrite as if you were setting aside cash flow for those eventual expenditures. In loans above $2 million, many lenders hold a reserve or impound account to ensure that funds are there when needed.

Now the lender has what they consider to be the borrower's likely cash available for mortgage payments, but the lender is conservative and wants to allow for the unexpected, so lenders build in further cushion. Different lenders will have various policies. In San Diego County, the most common rate has been 1.2:1. Banks want property to generate $120 of cash flow for every $100 of mortgage payment.

For the past 15 years, the underwriting math has worked out that borrowers would need a down payment of as low as 25% of the purchase price for "cash flow" for unglamorous or challenged or diverse zip codes. In more expensive zip codes like the beach or downtown, with more highly educated tenants, the borrower might need to put down 50% or more.

The Apartment Investing Realities chapter contains further discussion about why the fancy zip codes with the better educated, higher-credit-score tenants require larger down payments. The short version is that, even though fancier areas rent for more, investors pay an even greater premium to own in a fancy area than in a plain neighborhood. In San Diego County, beach zip codes can cost three times as much as "nightly news" zip codes.

Remember, interest rates vary. Low interest rates generally are more common during weaker economic times, and higher rates are associated with inflation and growth. When rents are increasing faster than average, inflation is usually higher than average, and interest tends to be higher.

Should you borrow at the cheaper floating rate or lock into the longest rate you can get, even though the price will be higher? I never know. The lenders set the rates, and then some buyers try to outsmart them. Unsophisticated people might think it is impossible to predict better than the international finance industry. The smartest person on the planet does not know the future. Your guess may be almost as good as the lenders'. We will all be wrong. Believe me, I have tracked forecasts for years. There is a cottage industry documenting how poorly experts do, in weather, politics, and economics.

I'm not suggesting you close your eyes and throw a dart at the board. However, there might be less stress with that option. I have no illusion of being able to offer any useful speculation about what the future rates will be.

Higher interest rates hurt the value of all income streams, and lower rates inflate the value of all income streams. Interest rates and the value of income streams are inversely related.

Appendix E

New Density Bonus Law Creates Powerful, but Temporary Profit Opportunity

THE DENSITY BONUS LAW IS THE LATEST government policy intended to mitigate California's rental housing shortage. The law will mitigate but not correct 30+ years of previous policy. The housing crisis is an unintended consequence of government policies.

The 2019 Density Bonus Law enables more housing, but many citizens will dislike the increased density. When government tries to resolve immense, complex, societal problems, "innocent bystanders" almost always suffer. Some people who gained in the previous system will lose privileges or bear costs in the revised reality. Such is life.

A few investors can earn superior returns by seizing this temporary opportunity. If you act on some little-understood realities, you can help correct our housing shortage and be outrageously rewarded. Learn how you might profit from this new law. This paper covers:

- California's Rental Housing Shortage
- Government's Imperfect Solution
- Your Temporary Opportunity

California's Rental Housing Shortage

About 40 states build enough housing for their citizens who rent. California policies permit enough executive homes and luxury condos. But California policies impose such high construction cost that developers can't earn a profit building rental housing for lower income households. Businesses don't deliberately seek losing ventures.

Houston's population is about one-fourth of California's population. **In the decade 2010–2019 Houston built more condos and apartments than California.** Consequently, both rents and apartments are relatively cheap in Houston. Both rents and apartments are relatively high in California. Here's why:

Local government policies make it more expensive to build apartments and condos in California than in Houston. In San Diego County the permits and fees can range from $30,000–$80,000 per apartment before any laborers appear on site. A Point Loma University study determined over 40% of the cost of San Diego County housing was due to permits, fees, and zoning requirements.

California divides sales tax with the jurisdiction where the sales occur. Every city in the state wants retail like car dealerships and shopping malls. Retail buildings worth $10 million generate sales tax revenue. They require relatively little fire, police, hospital, schools, water, or sewer services. Equal value apartments generate no sales tax but require more services than retail.

In layman's terms the local jurisdiction makes money by hosting retail but loses money by allowing apartments. Thus, every mayor in the state wants as much retail as they can get, and they want the city next door to build new apartments. By the way, the city next door wants all the same retail and wants none of the apartments. Local government has used zoning and impact fees to encourage retail and discourage rental housing.

The legislature didn't plan to discriminate against the poor. The unintended consequences of their policies caused the rental housing shortage. That has been true for more than 50 years.

The San Diego Association of Area Governments, SANDAG, reports San Diego County is 50,000+ rental units short of current population needs. If we doubled our apartment construction for 20 years, San Diego County would still have a rental housing shortage.

Government's (Imperfect) Solution

At the end of 2019 California passed its second Density Bonus Law with the objective of building more rental housing. State law prevails over every jurisdiction's zoning code and every homeowner association's conditions, covenants, and restrictions. The law has four significant provisions:

- Owner-occupied, single-family homes can now, by right, build an additional dwelling unit (ADU) of up to 1,200 square feet and a junior ADU of up to 400 square feet.

- Apartment buildings can convert existing nonresidential space, such as laundry rooms, storage, community centers, and attached garages or carports to 25% of the legal units. The local jurisdiction cannot require more parking.

- Each apartment parcel, if there is enough room, can also add two ADUs per parcel.

- The local jurisdiction has 60 days to approve the building plans.

The state's fanciest private community must abide by this law. Every exclusive community is bound by this law.

The governor and the legislature knew that California was not creating enough housing for the people in the lower half of the income scale. For more than a decade, cities ignored the state's calls to build their fair share of rentals, (i.e., significantly more rentals). Lawmakers considered several difficult trade-offs to get more housing built.

The law enables more housing. Some citizens will appreciate and others will resent the law. Lawmakers decided that people are more important than parking. In the future some homeowners might walk a half block from car to front door, as renters have done for years.

For years, lack of affordable rental housing made it too expensive for the men and women who grew up in San Diego to stay here, once they began to have a family. Thus, many local grandparents must travel to visit their grandchildren. More rental housing will enable more of those young families to stay in San Diego County.

Many grandparents will be happy to have the grandkids close by, even if grandma's kids, the grandkids' parents, must walk 50 more paces from car to home. Many grandparents will prefer not having to travel a day or two to get to see the grandkids.

Here's how the Density Bonus Law will affect rental housing and investor opportunity. I cite San Diego County numbers. The ratios will be similar throughout the state. The law sunsets in five years. Housing advocates hope it will be renewed then; we don't know whether it will be extended.

San Diego County has over 3 million people and over a million dwelling units. Roughly 450,000 are owner-occupied, single-family homes. The law would allow 900,000 additional residential units. My GUESS is less than 30,000 will be added to single-family home areas by end of 2024.

The single-family home parcels could host about 900,000 dwellings. All the apartment parcels combined could host about 60,000 more rentals. We won't be doubling our housing any time soon.

If 2% of the homeowners added ADUs in five years that could add 18,000 rentals. If 5% of the apartment potential is built that could be about 3,000 units. So, perhaps San Diego County might reduce our rental housing shortage in the next five years.

My guess is that three times more new rentals will be built in single-family neighborhoods as on apartment parcels. Single-family home areas might get 2–3% denser; multifamily areas might get 3–4% denser. Lawmakers chose this plan as the best way to provide more housing.

The California Density Bonus Law almost eliminates a local jurisdiction's ability to deny new residential construction. Thousands of homeowners will add granny flats; hundreds of homeowners will add a junior ADU. Thousands of rental owners will convert garages to create another studio or two.

It will take some time for the construction industry, lenders, and homeowners to understand the law and make financing and building ADUs easy. If 1% of the owner-occupied homes each year add a unit or two, that could add 5,000 new units per year to the rental housing stock.

Don't expect our county to eliminate our housing shortage. Maybe we'll stop falling behind. When San Diego had a million people, the city granted ONLY four building permits for granny flats. The city of San Diego, with a third of the county's population, is likely to allow 500 ADUs in 2020.

Let's consider why you might want to do it.

Your Temporary Opportunity

Changes create or expose opportunities. Some citizens dislike the law. In contrast a few investors will profit by seizing the opportunities. **Here's how it might work for you:**

Investors can create value by acquiring apartments with garages, then converting garages to housing. Careful construction can create value because the value of the extra rent should exceed the construction cost. Either be the builder or hire the builder. Investors buy income property for income. Investors pay a multiple of the annual rents.

As I write this, in 2020, few people in San Diego County recognize and are acting on this opportunity. That will change. In time the market will understand the impact of the Density Bonus Law and how to profit from it. The early adopters will have an immense advantage compared with those who only understand the option when best opportunities are gone. Here are some possible scenarios:

In 2019 builders paid $50,000–$100,000 per buildable apartment for land. Now apartments with extra land and those with attached garages and carports have the right to build extra rentals.

Before 2020 garages may have been worth $10,000–$15,000 each; now the garages might be worth $40,000–$50,000 each. Garages are frequently about 200 square feet. Two garages might become a studio; three garages might become a one-bedroom; four garages might become a two-bedroom.

Trade-offs are involved. Renters won't like fewer garage spaces and more people. Some entrepreneurial rental owners will stretch to obtain extra income. Some new units will have access via the side yard. Occasionally the main entrance might be via the alley.

Here's an example: Suppose you buy a fourplex with garages. An investor can obtain relatively more leverage, more bang per buck with a fourplex than a larger building.

San Diego County's typical fourplex has 30–70-year-old plumbing and electrical systems. Upgrade the fourplex's electrical, plumbing, and windows. This level of "substantial renovations" provides a temporary exemption from the 2019 rent control law. The existing rents can be reset to market when apartments rerent after upgrades. You can also convert four garages into another rental.

Converting garages to a rental might cost $40,000–$80,000 for construction and fees but might create $300,000 or more value. If the parcel has enough space, you could also add two more ADUs. For a specific minority of fourplexes, four rent checks could become seven.

A typical fourplex has at least two two-bedroom apartments. Two bedrooms rent for more than studios. Under the new law, you could add another two-bedroom unit from four garages.

Thoughtful analysis will be needed to determine which property type and which zip code will be most profitable. Knowledgeable experts will enable you to make better choices than trying to reinvent the wheel. Few people today understand the potential or the obstacles. Leverage, location, the local jurisdiction's cooperation, or obstinacy, and lot layout all affect the potential profitability of various options.

An 8-unit building with garages and enough land could be turned into 12 apartments. Two would be by right ADUs and two could be conversions of the garages. The extra rent could be 30% higher and might be worth $250,000+ profit after construction costs.

There are many details to work out. Every situation is different. This paper isn't an attorney's certification nor an architect's guarantee. Your results will vary depending on your specific asset, jurisdiction, skill, timing, and efficiency.

The biggest gains will be made by the people who act before most sellers and agents understand the opportunity and the value of the garages. Pioneers and innovators have more and better choices than settlers and late adopters.

Some investors will prosper and help resolve California's rental housing shortage. The largest profits will be made by the few investors who act most quickly. Two years from now thousands will understand what you're reading now. By 2025 this law will have expired.

This only sketches the possible opportunity. Contact your broker to find out more about your unique situation.

A Brief Annotated Reading List:
Wisdom from My Library

Increasing the Odds of Your Success

Essentialism: The Disciplined Pursuit of Less by Greg McKeown
This book's ideas are extremely important, and I'm still trying to master them. Choosing well is hard, and it can be harder as your choices and capacity increase. Focus on the fundamentals. Try to master the important first.

"Wrongology" Ted Talk by Katheryn Schulz
This 15-minute lesson has been among the most profound of my professional life. Most of us think that people who disagree with us are uninformed or stupid or wicked. That is false.

Emotional Intelligence: Why It Can Matter More Than IQ by Daniel Goleman
Almost all of us can improve in this vital arena.

The Luck Factor by Richard Wiseman
> Entertaining and useful.

Thinking Fast and Slow by Daniel Kahneman
> Most of us have sloppier thinking than we realize.

Rich Habits: The Daily Success Habits of Wealthy Individuals by Thomas Corley
> This quick read describes economic wisdom and economic folly. You'll see tangible examples of why some folks are rental owners and others will always be renters.

Misbehaving: The Making of Behavioral Economics by Richard H. Thaler
> Real people, not economic robots, not Mr. Spock, make financial choices.

Preparing to Invest Profitably

The SPEED of Trust: The One Thing That Changes Everything by Stephen M. R. Covey
> Not only is it nice to be nice, but there are economic rewards for treating people the way you want to be treated.

The Wealth Escalator

The Millionaire Next Door and *The Millionaire Mind* by Thomas Stanley, PhD
> These two books explain in granular detail who owns rentals: how they think and act. It is so easy, your history teacher may have done it.

How I Turned $1,000 into Five Million in Real Estate in My Spare Time by William Nickerson
> This classic is still relevant.

Getting to Yes: Negotiating Agreement without Giving In by Roger Fisher and William Ury

> Thousands consider this volume the best in its field.

Getting Past No: Negotiating in Difficult Situations by William Ury

> This follow-up shows how to win when the other side is hard to work with.

Great Courses: "The Art of Negotiating the Best Deal" by Seth Freeman

> Freeman builds gracefully and effectively on Fisher and Ury's classic.

Your Investment Life Trajectory

A Long Bright Future by Laura Carstensen

> We'll probably outlive our grandparents by a generation. Be happy, healthy, intentional, and fully alive in your bonus decades.

For Love & Money: A Comprehensive Guide to the Successful Generational Transfer of Wealth by Roy O. Williams

> Since you want to build a fortune, ensure that your family benefits from it and is not destroyed by it. Increase the odds that your legacy promotes your best values.

Other Valuable Books

Proverbs

> These slim pages have been in continuous print since the printing press was invented. More than a billion people have found wisdom here. A page a day can prevent folly and guide you to wisdom, regardless of whether you think the writing is inspired.

Crucial Conversations: Tools for Talking When the Stakes Are High by Kerry Patterson, Joseph Grenny, Ron McMillan, and Al Switzler
> All of us can be better communicators, especially when stakes are high and opinions differ. Model the best, not the worst or the just adequate.

Enough: True Measures of Money, Business, and Life by John Bogle
> Bogle applauds investors who earn an appropriate return for risking capital and enterprises which add value to society. He's disgusted by financial agents who have abandoned stewardship and focused on self-interest. His pages on professional vs. business are exemplary. I wish I had written them.

Nudge: Improving Decisions about Health, Wealth, and Happiness by Richard H. Thaler and Cass R. Sunstein
> You're a decision architect, whether you know it or not. Do it well, and scores of people around you will have better lives with little effort.

Still Surprised and *Reflections* by Warren Bennis
> Two books pointing out that you're a leader, whether you recognize it or not. We all learn by doing. You might as well do it well.

Triumph of the City: How Our Greatest Invention Makes Us Richer, Smarter, Greener, Healthier, and Happier by Edward Glaeser
> Our species' best invention can help your capital grow on steroids.

March of Folly by Barbara Tuchman
> This brilliant woman outlines how the world's most powerful blundered at global cost. You learn how to recognize and avoid less costly idiocy.

When the Boomers Bail by Mark Lautman

Outlines why thousands of communities are terrible places to invest. It provides indicators of which few areas may be able to overcome massive difficulties.

Additional Resources

A SPECIAL WEBSITE provides additional resources to support you as you apply the lessons in this book. You'll find the site at:

https://BuildingLegacyWealth.com

Acknowledgments

THE PEOPLE ACKNOWLEDGED HEREIN have shown a commitment to living lives worth imitating; they recognize and embrace their calling. Each cares about others and has demonstrated acting on wisdom, being courageous, living out sacrificial love, seeking excellence, speaking the truth in love, and other traits I admire and aspire to. More than one of them aspire to "Do the right thing, and then one more." Each has challenged, invited, or modeled unique paths of deeper excellence. A few don't aspire to material wealth; not many are brokers; most are not in business.

In alphabetical order by last name, I thank:

Denise Bailey; Nick Bailey; Gary Barnes; Javonda Barnes; Ann Block, CCIM; Mindy Bortness; Jim Brondino, CCIM; Roger Brown, CCIM, PhD; Mike Chasin; Alan Chiyatat; Walt Clements, CCIM; John Colclough; Stacey Coleman, OD; Jeanie Davis; Don Eklund; Dan Feder; Joe Greenblatt, CPM; Norm Hamlin; Bill Hanna; Walt Henrichsen; Dwight Hill; Chuck Hoffman; Duane Horning, Esq.; Birgitta Hufnagel, MD; Margaret Hulter,

Esq.; Gayle Jackson; Dave Jones; R. J. Kelly; Tom Liguori; Lucinda Lilley, CPM; Gary London; Bill McCurrine, Esq.; Deb Moncaukas, PhD; Rick Moncaukas; Bill Moore; Sue Moore; Tom Morgan, CCIM; Don Mosher; Karen Nelson; Calvin Nolan; Emmett Pinney; Dick Roberts; Mark Roberts; Rod Santomassimo, CCIM; Amy Selby; John Sheehan, AIA; Carol Slomka; Mark Slomka; Pete Smith, CPM; Kim Snider; Norm Snider; Leslie Spiess; Scott Spiess; Al Stahl; Lynn Stahl; and Blaine Strickland, CCIM.

Equally important for opposite reasons are dozens of nameless others who provided clear and tangible examples of the cost of ego, folly, and greed: what not to think, say, or do.

Special thanks and acknowledgement go to current and alumni star teammates Kiley Berlinksi, Ian Couwenberg, Charline Gnangbe, Barry Herbst, Teresa Miller, and Paul Peszt. They helped explore, discover, and implement ways to seek excellence in our imperfect craft.

You, gentle reader, owe more than you realize to Wally Bock, my writing coach, who culled out more than half to leave only what we hope has been worth your time, while refining what might benefit you. For many months he has labored for your benefit and befriended me. When he says "No," I smile and thank him.

Finally, the most important two are patient, and wise: Sandy, bride of my youth, and Jesus, for accepting, challenging, correcting, forgiving, inspiring, and loving me. They model how to love God and love others.

About Terry Moore, CCIM

TERRY MOORE HELPS REAL ESTATE INVESTORS make the most important financial choice of their next decade. He's a top apartment broker who has received ten major recognitions, including Investment Broker of the Year, Deal Maker of the Year, Transaction of the Year, and CCIM of the Year. In January 2018, Terry received the inaugural Commercial Broker of the Year award from the San Diego Association of Realtors.

Terry has long advocated improving property. Over the years, nearly 100,000 residents have lived in apartments that were upgraded by his clients. All of his group investments made money for his investors. Each property he and Sandy have owned was in better shape when they disposed of the asset than when the property was acquired.

After earning his MBA at Southern Methodist University, Terry worked for the world's largest bank, owned a hardware store, was a shopping center developer, and then became a hyperactive income property broker.

Terry has been a commercial broker since 1987. He earned the CCIM (Certified Commercial Investment Member) designation, which has been awarded to fewer than 5% of commercial investment brokers. He has been a member of the national CCIM faculty.

Terry's articles have been published in national, state, regional, and local magazines. He wrote the "Trusted Advisor" column in the *San Diego Daily Transcript* and frequently contributes articles to the San Diego County Apartment Association's *Rental Owner.*

He summited Kilimanjaro at 59 and took up triathlons after 60. In his spare time, he is on track to read 50 nonfiction books this year.

Terry is an owner of ACI Apartment Consultants Inc., San Diego's most effective apartment brokerage firm.

Terry and Sandy have been married 40 years, have been rental owners for 37 of those years, and have been working in the same business daily for most of their marriage. They enjoy active living in San Diego, which will likely include more triathlons, as well as hiking in and out of the Grand Canyon again. Between them, they often read 100 books annually.